W9-BVZ-505

Candace,

Bless you and your ministry! Now is truly your time!

Now is the Time

How to Recover and Reap During Times of Recession

C.C. Harrison

Copyright © 2011 by C.C. Harrison

Now is the Time
How to Recover and Reap in Times of Recession
by C.C. Harrison

Printed in the United States of America

ISBN 9781612155388

www.xulonpress.com

DEDICATION

To God, my father—you are the creator of all things! Thank you for ideas, insights, income, and integrity.

As I write this page of acknowledgement to the ones I love, I am extremely aware that it may be the most important page of this book. Were it not for your constant support and encouragement, none of the other pages would follow.

To my parents, Benjamin Clay and Ethel Clay—I owe you all. Thank you for making me believe I could do anything. To Ben, my brother—what awesome gifts you have. I love you much, and I am so proud to be your "BIG" sister.

I salute and honor my spiritual parents, Bishop Lester Love and Pastor Fran Love. Without your love and guidance, I would not have dreamed bigger and better dreams. Thanks for showing me what excellence and persistence look like. And to Richard Berry of Century 21... thanks for teaching me how to set goals and sell houses. Because of you, I have faith, courage, and enthusiasm!

AND FINALLY

To my husband and children—Michael, Michael II, and Tayler—you give me love and inspiration unconditionally. I can't say enough how very proud and grateful I am for you all. Because you exist, my purpose in life is already fulfilled. You all mean the world to me.

TABLE OF CONTENTS

FOREWORD

BY BISHOP LESTER LOVE

When I was in a transitional time on the business side of my career, I needed someone to take the reigns and guide the ship to a safe destination. We were going through tough financial times, and I knew that my education and expertise had taken us as far as we could go. I could not afford to lose momentum. And now after over 10 years, I thank God everyday for sending me C.C. Harrison.

Besides being a trustworthy confidant, an extremely loyal and qualified leader; she has the perfect balance between smarts, personal experience and common sense to show us how to thrive during challenging times. C.C. is the primary reason why I am experiencing the level of success I am in our ministry and business. I have relied on her financial savvy which has guided us through the rough times and lean seasons, and we always came out on top. Her wisdom will show you how to experience goals you have always wanted in your finances. Through the practical principles of *Now is the Time*, you will see results previously only dreamed of in no time.

C.C. is my financial consciousness as I'm sure after reading this treasure and applying these incredible strategies to your life, she will be yours. You are about to begin a journey that you will never forget, and like me, you will thank God everyday for C.C. Harrison.

Lester Love

ix

PREFACE

Amidst turbulent financial times and unstable economic environments, reports of governmental bailout plans, frozen credit markets, and corporate downsizing become familiar mainstays of the daily news. Make no mistake about it, America is in a recession, and it has been for quite some time. The last few months of the year 2007 marked the beginning of economic turmoil and pushed the country into a recession that has everyone scrambling to find answers. What is the cause of our broken and ailing economy?

While many are pointing fingers in attempts to assign blame for the country's current condition, we are gravely aware that most will be affected by the crisis. Whether through decreasing housing markets, home foreclosures, job loss, or investment scams, everyone is concerned about steps to take in order to get the economy moving again. Worry and fear have no doubt gripped the minds of countless Americans who have recently learned that their hard-earned life savings and retirement plans are no longer there.

For some, it may seem like a nightmare or the end of the world as they learn of their financial fate. It's the kind of feeling that overtakes a patient who goes to the physician's office for a routine check up, but leaves with a heart-wrenching diagnosis of a terminal illness. How's the prognosis? How much time do I have left? How could this happen to me? These are just a few of the questions that may arise as the individual tries to find a cause for the disease that will inevitably change their way of living and thinking. No doubt, changes will come as the attending physician devises a treatment

xi

plan in efforts to combat the disease and thwart untoward signs and symptoms precipitating the progression of the disease.

Well our economy is no different. Many of us were going about our daily lives assuming that all was well. Until one day, all the talk of the worsening economy caused us to stop and take an assessment of our condition. All of the negative reports in the news, a friend's lay-off, or monthly financial statements with a decreasing 401K balance have prompted us to take a closer look at our fiscal health; and the prognosis may not be what we thought it would. The diagnosis is a recession related to over-spending and excessive consumption of resources.

As of this writing, the biggest financial rip-off in history, executed by Bernard Madoff, was recently revealed as he bilked over $50 billion dollars from unwitting investors with a scam that would leave anyone "sick to the stomach." Reports of the devastation are far-reaching, and even the wealthiest of our society were victims to his invasion. Yes, even the financially strong became susceptible to a scam that eventually unraveled and left the would-be investors with bad news.

As we listen to the nightly news and read the economic reports and articles, some of the things—we may be able to follow. But then, there are certain concepts that leave us puzzled and confused. We have no idea what they are talking about. What has really happened? What's going on now? And what does it mean for me? While we may not understand all of what the economists are talking about, we do know one thing. When we see that big red arrow facing south on the television screen as they report on the stock market, we know it can't be good. Consequently, I found myself wondering more and more about the personal implications of the recession. I figured I'd better get some answers and find the meaning within it all. So for those of you who were also wondering, here it is:

A recession, simply stated, is...
"A period of decreased economic activity"

What happens during a recession is this: people and businesses generally conserve, and they tend not to freely spend or lend as they would during normal or active economic periods. Employers are forced to evaluate their resources and use them wisely as they cut unnecessary spending in order to minimize waste. As a result, millions of workers are inevitably laid off, and unemployment soars throughout corporations large and small. Sadly, that's where America has found herself after recent years of excessive spending. We are overwhelmed with the bad news, so naturally all we want is a pain-numbing shot in the arm and another band-aid so that we may feel better about our fiscal health.

This book is not about the bad news regarding our economy. Although the prognosis is definitely not good, there is good news. There is hope, and the recession is not the end of the world or the end of your life. There are still measures to take and goals which may be achieved if you all willing to stay in the battle. Yes, you are wounded, but as long as you are alive, there is hope to recover, restore, and rebuild better than before.

If you are anything like me, you have spent countless hours seeking a way out of the rat race and bondages of a depleted budget. You know what it feels like to seriously ask yourself, "How can I get out of this rut and hopeless situation that seems to be sucking the life out of me?" If this is the case, this book is for you. If you are tired of going after every seminar and falling for the wealth-building gurus who come to take even more of the money you don't have only to leave you with no practical answers, this book is definitely for you. I have been there, and I know that the answer is not in using the same old habits and techniques. If you are going to make it through tough and faltering economic times, now is the time to do something differently in order to gain different results. The following precepts are presented in a straight forward format. They will cause you to look at your situation differently and compel you to take immediate action so that the healing process can begin.

CHAPTER 1

A TIME FOR THE EMERGENCY ROOM

Have you ever experienced a medical emergency? If you have, you know how chaotic it can be. There is a bit of uncertainty and fear related to the unknown as you encounter an urgent situation requiring medical attention from emergency personnel. Embedded within the preface, you may have noticed a bit of reference to medical terminology throughout my description of the economy. There is a reason for this approach, and I will share with you why.

Prior to becoming an administrator, realtor or investor, I had been, by profession, a registered nurse for several years. During which time, I worked mainly in hospice and geriatric care. I have had the opportunity to see the life-long effects of excessive behaviors that ultimately led to the demise of my patients. Years of smoking and bad eating habits resulted in cancer, diabetes, hypertension and other life-threatening diseases. All of which led the patients to us for treatment or some type of palliative care.

Although scores of them had gone their entire lives without so much as a single physical, here they were fighting to survive every day with as little pain or drug side effects as possible. Engaged in a battle for their health, they had all been given a diagnosis, and each individual's prognosis was not good. They needed treatment to live or at least to achieve the best quality of life attainable.

It was a pleasure to be involved in their treatment and to offer whatever assistance I could to make them feel better and to offer them hope to go on. I was able to help them because I had prepared for their situation. Even though they were diagnosed with critical diseases, there was always the possibility of full recovery and remission from their acute conditions. The ones who pulled through were the individuals who found something within to keep them going. They would not give up hope, but rather they would follow the treatment plans to the letter in order to get better and get on with their lives— even if others around them had given up hope. We call them the "survivors". While everyone else had accepted the "bad news" and caved in at the initial diagnosis, the survivors took in the facts, learned whatever they could about the disease process, and continued to live their best lives. The "survivors" are able to move pass what's happening in their lives and think about all of the possibilities and opportunities that still await them. Somehow, it never enters their thoughts that they may not make it through. On the contrary, they are excited about what they will achieve once this period in their lives is over. No matter what happens, they go on to emerge stronger and lead more productive, positive lives.

This book is about living your best life, and proceeding pass the prognosis and current economic challenges of our day with a positive attitude; however there is a plan to follow in order to get better and achieve the greatest quality of life possible. There is a perfect plan for recovery as we seek to redefine our faith in God, our joy in family, and our desire to take control over finances. These are the most important things in life, and if you are reading this book, you undoubtedly want to do something about your life or your present status. Maybe because you realize that there is a problem somehow. Although you can't quite put your finger on it, there is perhaps an uneasy feeling that something is internally wrong; and you need to find out what's going on. Sure, you've been able to ignore the signs and symptoms for some time now, but lately they have gotten worse, and fear has you motivated to seek help. It's time for a trip to the emergency room, because you can no longer ignore what's troubling you and causing you pain or discomfort.

WE HAVE AN EMERGENCY!

It's no secret that many emergency room personnel cite pain as a primary factor and reason why most people proceed to the hospital emergency room. During an initial interview, triage nurses usually ask several questions in attempts to ascertain what brought the patient in for this particular visit. Some incidences of the emergency room include victims of motor vehicular accidents or serious childhood accidents causing severe trauma or injuries, violent crime insults, chest pain, or acute cold and flu symptoms. While these incidences represent the most common reasons individuals seek immediate medical attention, there are still others who come to the emergency room after chronic pain and discomfort intensifies in an area previously ignored or tolerated. The sufferer ultimately comes in because they could no longer go on without addressing the issue.

Unfortunately, the latter cases would result in the inevitable news of a disease that had exacerbated past the possibility of effective treatment. At which time, the patient would require consultations or opinions from specialists and expensive modalities of prolonged treatments with hopes of curative outcomes. Many times, the very treatments prescribed to counteract the disease would soon affect other systems and body functions thereby causing untoward side effects and discomfort. Consequently, the patients and their caregivers would respond in one of two ways. They would either give up—refusing to undergo the extensive treatments and cite extreme difficulty in completing the regimen they had started. Most likely, these were the sufferers who had put off a trip to the emergency room because they were too busy or too afraid to face what was causing their ailments. They had undoubtedly convinced themselves that if they ignored the problems, somehow the problems would disappear or get better without intervention.

Usually, when there is an underlying issue or problem within our physical bodies, there is always some type of way to mask the initial signs and symptoms. Only the individual knows of the increasing incidences of headaches or fatigue, which is generally a sign of a more serious disease such as high blood pressure or diabetes. However, if nothing is done to prevent, treat, or otherwise address the causative factors—the issue progresses with greater and more intense occurrences within the body until it ultimately affects other connecting systems.

Because the body seeks constant balance, it will initially compensate for the defective system or organ, but only for so long. After prolonged periods of compensation without relief, the system would eventually fail from over-exertion therefore leading to the depletion, exhaustion, and final shut-down of the system. If you are thinking "bankruptcy" here, then you are right on target, and you now understand what happened to our economy.

Although the political insiders and economists warned of impending economic collapse, the symptoms and warnings went unheeded— or should I say *"untreated"* until the devastation overwhelmed our infrastructure sending shock waves to Wall Street, as well as Main Street. We now have individual households and families resorting to foreclosure and bankruptcy as the only coping mechanism for their exorbitant debt. If this isn't bad enough, some of those who will be affected didn't even cause the breakdown, but are now being affected just because of a connection to the system.

The problem went unnoticed while America's leaders closed their eyes to a malfunctioning and broken market instead of dealing with the catastrophe like the emergency it was. Picture the patients who postponed desperately needed urgent care treatments thinking that it would "work out" without intervention. Unfortunately, these cases happen very often because people tend not to head to the emergency room until the problems they face are so severe that they have no other choice. Most individuals don't see the urgency in their situations until it's usually too late. They wait too long, but when they finally show up... it's an emergency, and they want help right away. Sure they have been dealing with the ailments for years, and they have been forewarned of the detrimental threats of going untreated, but we now have an emergency!

We have all seen the hospital-based dramas and sitcoms on television. Although very entertaining and thrilling at times, many scenes portray those who are in this very situation, and they require an entire team to diagnose and treat them. The circumstances make for a serious dilemma, and the team is compelled to relentlessly work at developing a plan to cure the suffering soul. Often times, the team must be creative in their therapeutic approaches though the patient's condition is severe, and the crisis is impending.

Emergency dramas are rousing, and the actors, writers, and directors really have a way of entertaining us with realistic, true-to-life presentations. I especially enjoy the shows that combine drama, suspense, and a bit of comedy for the viewing pleasure of their audiences. According to The Neilsen Company, the leading media research corporation in the U.S., of the top 10 Broadcast TV programs for the first month of 2009, two (2) hospital-based programs helped their networks to retain high ratings with a combined, estimated 30 million viewers each week tuning in to view *Grey's Anatomy* at position #7 and the 9th ranked *House* (http://www.nielsenmedia.com, February 2, 2009).

The statistical ratings of the "made-for-television" dramas are favorable as millions of viewers tune in to watch the award-winning casts. While I, like many others, am impressed by these statistics, I realize that our nation's economy is no television drama. We are not viewers, but rather, we are all participants each holding a substantial stake in what happens during this economic crisis. Our 44th President, Barack Obama is not a celebrity or star, although he was described as such by a few of his critics. I think we all realize that television is television, and it's just "make believe" with characters who don't really deal with the depicted circumstances as we see them.

We are facing a real situation in America, and the possibility for recovery depends upon our ability to develop a plan of action. As I mentioned before, we did not suddenly get into this crisis, so it will be difficult to break the cycle of debt overnight. It is true that it has been a long time coming, and if the struggle with debt is going to end, we will be required to change our entire culture and way of thinking. If we are truly going to recover and walk in abundance, we must first deal with the debt struggle.

THE DEBT STRUGGLE

Struggling with debt is a horrible feeling. Ask anyone who has ever been there, and they will tell you that it often makes you feel like you need to take a trip to the emergency room. The signs are shortness of breath or tightness in the chest, headaches, anxiety attacks, depression, fatigue, and dizziness—and that's just a few of the symptoms. I am sure that there are many other very real and substantial physical effects that you or I have experienced related to the debt struggle. Let's face it, when debt collectors are calling and adding to the pressure of your lack, it genuinely affects you and makes you feel like you have a "bonafide" emergency. If someone doesn't step in to help or revive you, you are going to lose it!

Does this sound like fear taking control? Certainly it is fear at its best, and it grips you almost as though you are having a heart attack. You know it does not feel good. I'll admit it if you won't. It makes you feel desperate and powerless, and I'm not ashamed to admit that I have been there. You try to keep everything positive and clear your mind of all the negative thoughts of bankruptcy, foreclosure, mounting unpaid bills; but nothing seems to work. Something has to happen if you are going to make it through with your mind intact. It's terrifying, and the body responds in a "fight or flight" syndrome as it tries to survive in the midst of the attack.

Garrett Sutton, in his insightful book, *The ABC's of Getting Out of Debt,* writes of the physiological and psychological effects of debt: "Everyone in debt knows that debt can make you feel sick. You plan around it; you think about it; you worry about it. Many of us can trace our level of stress right back to our level of debt."

It's no wonder that many people feel as though they cannot deal with it, and they tend to give up and stop trying. They give in to depression taking on an attitude of indifference and self-destruction. The stress is so hard to bear, and no amount of alcohol or drugs or pain pills will numb the feelings or fix the problem.

If you are currently in this position, your situation is severe, and it's time to ask for help! Drastic circumstances call for drastic measures, so do something you have never done before. Ask for help so that you won't have to fight alone. Debt-related stress and pressure has been known to cause people to act frantically and resort to dreadful actions such as suicide or mental breakdowns. It's time to take a trip to the emergency room whereby you may be inspired and resuscitated such as the patients we view on the hospital television dramas.

I sense that people are hurting as the recession will cause difficulty for many individuals and families facing issues of job loss and lack of resources; but allow me to give you the inspirational advice you need to take back your life. Take a minute to clear your mind and regroup so that you won't suffer a stroke. There is always hope as long as there is breath in your body. With God's help, you can start all over again, because He is the author and finisher of your faith. He can breathe life into your dead situation and cause you to prosper and be in good health. Though you are in over your head right now because of the mistakes and bad decisions you made in the past, He is the God of *"another chance"*, and He will get you out of this one too.

COPING VS. CONQUERING

In addition to knowing that God will work out your situation, you must also act at this time. Please believe me...Now is the best time to recover, rebuild, and reap. It's not enough to say or think about getting out, but you need to get up and *DO SOMETHING*. It's high time you stopped *coping* with your condition or situation. It's time to start *conquering* your situation, and there is definitely a difference. I will share with you how.

Those who cope with an issue are merely tolerating the present condition, and they tend to adapt to the stressful environment by working within the confines of negative situations. People who cope are in bondage, but they tend to find the positive points related to their struggle. Ask any person addicted to alcohol, gambling, or any other addiction; and they will tell you that they are not as bad off as it seems. They cope with the bondage because they like the way it makes them feel.

Conquering, however, is an entirely different approach. To conquer means *to overcome; to triumph over; or to take control of* as *by defeat*. Now doesn't that sound like a better alternative? Debt is the enemy or stronghold here, and we must see it from this point of view. If debt is causing you feelings of fear, powerlessness and depression, it is the same as a person whom you fear. As an enemy, debt must be conquered in order for you to walk away victoriously. Don't

21

just think about getting out. Think about winning the fight. I don't just want to get out or debt. I want financial freedom with enough abundance to help others to get out. I know it may sound strange to suggest that you give to others when you may not have enough to pay all of your debts. I agree that it may be bizarre to propose, but it has been ironically demonstrated by a great majority of successful people. Those who operate in abundance and wealth enthusiastically bear witness that it may be attributed to their generosity.

When you are ready to conquer your feelings of anxiety and fear regarding not having enough, try giving a portion of what you have to someone else in need. You will soon feel a sense of accomplishment and satisfaction that is hard to describe or explain. Just recently, I found myself in a situation of a financial short-fall, and I did not have enough to meet all of my monthly obligations. Instead of feeling sorry for myself or allowing fear to grip me, I decided to take what I had and donate a portion of it to St. Jude Children's Hospital. I felt that it was a worthy cause to which I could contribute, and I was sure that my donation would help someone to go on, even if it was just for one more day. The feeling I received upon mailing that check was greater than worrying about my debt. I had no doubt that I would later receive a ten-fold return on what I had given, and I told myself that I would pay my bills later when I got the return.

I felt empowered as I made the decision to control my situation. The money or financial situation did not control me, but I controlled what I had in my possession. That's the best weapon over powerlessness. The key is to take control of what you can control, and make a decision to do what you can do. Maybe I could not afford to pay the $2,000 toward a bill that month, but I could control and offer a percentage of what I needed to a worthy cause to help someone else get closer to their goal. I would be remiss if I didn't tell you that within less than a week… I received the $2,000 plus an extra $4,398.00.

It's now time to do something to get out and conquer your bad situation. Use the energy of pain and frustration to your advantage to ***DO SOMETHING***. An unexpected lay-off or sudden loss of income tends to be just the right stimulus in compelling us to re-define who we are and what we want out of life. Let's be clear. Now is not the time to allow your circumstance to hold you back from achieving your dreams.

DO SOMETHING FOR YOU

If you are one of countless Americans recently laid off, you may need to take some much needed time to step away from your everyday routine and look from the outside—in. Sometimes it's hard to take an accurate assessment when we are directly in the midst of an issue because we're too busy doing, and running, and getting, and taking care of the business—well, you get the picture. Consequently, one day, we stop to notice that we are too overwhelmed to enjoy any of the fruits of our labor. Our priorities somehow got mixed in with making money to support our excessiveness, and suddenly, there was no place or time for our God-given gifts or passions. Maybe this is the time to re-discover you. Why not use the extra time as a long-awaited vacation in which you reward yourself with time alone, time with family, or time with God. Consider what makes you happy and what makes you tick.

In a featured article found in Jet Magazine (April 20-27, 2009), career coach and author, Delatorro McNeal advises those who have recently been forced out of employment to take an inventory of your talents, abilities and skills. He further suggests that you broaden your skills in order to compete within the job market, and 'ask yourself what do you really want to be doing with your life?' It's important here to really get clear and start to think about the things that matter most to you.

There are all types of support and debt management resources, and here's where you may want to start. The following steps may be the difference between life and death for your financial, and yes, maybe even your physical survival as it relates to conquering the debt struggle. It's not too late for you, and the economy is not so bad for you to come out on top. You can beat the disease of debt and its infectious effects on your life although it has become very contagious in our society. I did it by changing my mindset regarding debt and credit and by changing my perception of what is going on with the economy. It's the only way to make any real change in your life. You have to look at things differently and check your beliefs and perceptions of the world systems which have caused you to end in a place of detriment.

In author, Joe Vitale's best-selling book, *The Attractor Factor*, he suggests..."The beliefs you have create the results you get." What does this mean? Well, it infers that if are getting negative results, you must check your beliefs. If you are constantly experiencing lack, then this may be an area in your life where your belief pattern is altered or somehow out of line.

It may be time to check your greatest struggle or the problems of your past. In which areas are you failing? If it's a recurring, financial struggle, maybe you have a deficiency in the way you were taught to deal with money. If that is the case, then you have to change years and years of patterns or habits that probably originated with your parents. I remember reading a story in Suze Orman's *The 9 Steps to Financial Freedom* in which she detailed a most traumatic experience of her childhood. She described the catastrophe of a fire destroying her family's business. Amazingly, she remembers her father running into the blazing building to save the cash register inside. After safely escaping the fire, he impulsively ran back into the inferno to carry out what amounted to their only means of savings and income. He evidently was not as afraid of being burned to death as he faced the fear of losing all of the cash register's contents. Her views regarding money were established at that point as she thought… "Money is obviously more important than life itself." She has been on a financial quest to help others deal with their fears and anxieties regarding money ever since.

Perhaps you are not in a financial battle, but if there is any uncertainty or anxiety in your life about anything, you will experience signs and symptoms of uneasiness in the area of your struggle. This is usually an area where you are highly skilled or passionate, but there always seems to be something out of sync. You are fundamentally productive in the area of this struggle, but something continues to hold you back from getting the breakthrough or real release to flourish. Could it be that you are not clear on what it is you truly want?

Joe Vitale also suggests that you "get clear" on what you want to be, do, or have in your life. Then—and only then can you find your way to wholeness, happiness, and a life fulfilled. Anything short of a life fulfilled, is a life filled with lack. You may not be in the group that we spoke of earlier, and maybe you are not yet at the point of depression or powerlessness. But rather, you are at the point of stress and disappointment due to a loss of control. Your situation may not indicate a trip to the emergency room, but it's likely a good time for a check- up.

CHAPTER 2

TIME FOR A CHECK UP

In order to really get clear on what you want, your first step should be geared toward gaining singleness of mind. Your focus is to weed out all of the unnecessary stuff. Clear those negative thoughts out of your mind by focusing on what you really want.

Think of yourself as a gardener who has been hired to clear away weeds from a client's most prized garden. You will want to cut away or prune all of the wild flowers that make the space unattractive. This will take some work, but you must focus on your goal, and that is to get rid of the undesirable plants or the unwanted aspects that are growing and overtaking the beautiful ones. The desirable flowers can only bloom when they are free and clear to grow in a favorable habitat. Will they grow as long as the weeds are present? Yes, they will, but their true beauty will not be realized, and you will not truly reap a great-looking garden unless you check what's blocking them.

WHAT'S BLOCKING YOU FROM BLOSSOMING?

Is there something holding you from reaching your full potential? Take the time to check what has been troubling you, and deal with it. What are your complaints at this time? Once you change the way you think about your complaints or your greatest struggles, you are on your way to recovery. My pastor and spiritual father, Bishop Lester Love says it like this: *"Check your troubles."* There, you will

26

usually find the area of your greatest gift or anointing, and that's the area where the enemy wants to attack you. Your adversary wants to terminate your strongest points before you even get started, and if he can frustrate you with problems and troubles, he can stop you. So, how did you get to the place of disappointment and frustration? If you want to know the meaning of it all, your solution has to begin with the first step in a detailed process.

God wants us to be clear in our thinking in order to be productive and grow. There is no lack in Him, nor is there any lack in our universe. He is the creator of all things and all beings, so since He made us, He knows all about us. He knows our short-comings. He knows our past failures, our mistakes, and our broken areas. Someone once said… "If you want to know the purpose of a creation, then ask the creator." So at this point, it is essential for us to remember our Creator and ask Him for the wisdom that we need in order to handle every problem that exasperates us. We just need to be clear on what it is we are dealing. We need Godly wisdom to help us identify the problems we face and what we should do to escape. Even if you are unsure of where you are or what you really want to achieve, God is able to help you.

If you need wisdom—if you want to know what God wants you to do—
ask Him, and He will gladly tell you. He will not resent your asking.

But when you ask Him, be sure that you really expect Him to answer,
For a doubtful mind is as unsettled as a wave of the sea that is driven
and tossed by the wind

People like that should not expect to receive anything from the Lord.
They can't make up their minds; they waver back and forth in
everything they do.

James 1:5-8—New Living Translation

So make sure that you take the time to deal with that which clutters and blocks you from reaching your full potential. Then, and only then, can you concentrate on specifically what you want out of life.

BE SPECIFIC

God deals in specifics, and numbers, and measurements; so I believe He wants us to be specific in our approaches and our requests. This is just His way, and it's how He gets things done. When He told Noah to build the ark, He gave him specific measurements. When He told Solomon to build the temple, He gave specific, numeric measurements. Again, God is specific in what He does, and He operates within systematic approaches to accomplish everything in the earth realm. He is waiting on us to be specific in our requests and to operate within His order. We can request whatever we desire, but we must get clear on where we are and what we truly want. By knowing what you don't want (current problems or complaints), you will be able to identify and ascertain what you do want.

Most times, we do not achieve what we would like to see in our lives because we aren't specific in identifying the problem. If we are experiencing financial lack, we just ask for increase when we make our requests because we think that more money will somehow solve all of our problems. We ask for increase, but we are seldom specific enough as to how much we need. We just simply state…"Increase". Well everybody wants an increase, so what makes your case so different? Why can't you get clear on exactly how much you need in order to experience total financial freedom?

Instead, we just vaguely ask for increase. Increase in what area? Do you want an increase in bills or headaches? Do you need an increase in sleepless nights? You want to reap, but what do you want to reap? Look at it this way. When you are hungry, you don't just go into a restaurant and say, "Give me food." You order precisely what you would like to eat, and they bring it to your table as you ordered it. Even if they fail to get the order right, it doesn't matter. You have the right to command specifically what you want again until you receive it. Now I'm not suggesting here that God is some type of waiter or bus-boy waiting on you to order; but He is the owner and ruler of all things, and He offers them to us freely. He employs angels who act on His behalf, and they may be petitioned to go to and fro in the fulfillment of our specific requests. Once I decided I was tired of being in debt, I wrote out all of my debt in a table of creditors, account balances, and monthly payments. After assessing my situation, I was able to write and request the exact amount that I needed. My prayers became really specific as I started to cry out for exactly **$85,701.55!** I even made a chart of everything I would do with the money if God released it to me, and I logged it in with dates and amounts as I received it. Pretty soon, I started to see the money coming in from strange places. Within 4 months, I had received nearly 2/3 or 75% of the money I requested.

Now I know what you are thinking... If God is "all-knowing" and omnipresent, why am I required to ask Him for what I need? Doesn't He already know? What a great point! But here's an even greater point. Yes, God knows exactly what you need, but remember that His ways are not our ways; and His thoughts are not our thoughts. He already knows the plan that He has towards you. Consequently, God already knows you want more money in order that you might experience happiness and peace, so His thought is... Why don't I just give you peace? We equate financial abundance to happiness, but He already knows that He can give you so much more than money to make you happy. He wants to give you what money can not buy.

As I stated earlier, there is no lack in Him. Even if there is a deficit in the economy, He can still cause you to operate in abundance. So you've lost a few things. Remember He is the source of it all, and He can replenish or replace everything that concerns you. You can recover it all as He supplies you with the necessary tools you need to bounce back.

And My God shall supply all your need
according to His riches in glory by Christ Jesus.

Philippians 4:19 — New King James Version

He wants to meet your need, however in calculating how much you require, also try to figure out why you want it. Is the problem with money a result of poor spending habits? If so, your problem can never be resolved with just a request for more money. Your aim should include a check-up to see why you are having trouble with money. You've got to get specific in order to devise a plan, and the only way

29

you could know the specifics about the issue at hand, is to stop and check your perception of what seems to be ailing you. We will cover the specifics of how to perform an assessment, because recovery doesn't just start when the problem disappears. It starts with an assessment. However, for now, we have to know what's the problem?

It is also important to realize here that you are not the only one who has ever faced your area of difficulty or experienced a problem before. There is nothing new under the sun, but the enemy wants you to feel hopeless and full of despair as you confront your situation believing that you are alone in what you face. But nothing could be further from the truth. Just as you are not alone in your experience, this nation as well as many other nations have gone through recessions in the past. It even dates as far back as biblical days in which they witnessed horrible famines in the land. They too were forced to participate in a process of systematic approach in order to overcome.

Here's how King Pharaoh and the Egyptians got through it and came out victoriously. As you read on, you will begin to see how God was able to change Pharaoh's perception and cause him to check what was troubling him.

Then the seven years of plenty which were in the land of Egypt ended, and the seven years of famine began to come, as Joseph had said. The famine was in all lands, but in all the land of Egypt there was bread.

So when all the land of Egypt was famished, the people cried to Pharaoh for bread. Then Pharaoh said to all the Egyptians, "Go to Joseph; whatever he says to you, do."

The famine was over all the face of the earth, and Joseph opened all the storehouses and sold to the Egyptians. And the famine became severe in the land of Egypt.

So all countries came to Joseph in Egypt to buy grain, because the famine was severe in all lands.

Genesis 41:53-56—New King James Version

As the king and ruler of Egypt, it's easy to comprehend that Pharaoh had a situation, and he needed a revelation. So he called Joseph, the dreamer with hopes that he would be able to interpret two dreams that had been troubling him. First, Pharaoh dreamed of seven, fatted cows gazing in the pastures then seven, lean or ill-favored cows came up behind them and ate up the seven well-favored or fatted cows. Pharaoh then goes back to sleep, and he dreamed a second time of seven ears of corn sprouting up on one stalk; but then there were seven thin ears of corn that later sprouted up and came to devour the seven rank and full ears.

It was a dream, but it troubled Pharaoh, and he wanted to know what was the meaning of all this? What's really going on? So he calls a little slave boy— Joseph, a prisoner from Canaan to interpret his dream. Joseph tells him that the two dreams are one in the same. God is trying to show Pharaoh what he is about to do, and He's going to do it in a short time. However, God is gracious enough to show him twice. Joseph's interpretation reveals that the seven fatted cows and the seven rank and full ears of corn represent seven years of plenty in which the people of Egypt would experience abundance and prosperity unlike they ever had before.

The seven skinny cows and the seven thin ears of corn that came to devour the full ears of corn represent famine. So Egypt would experience seven years of great prosperity in which the earth would bring forth handfuls of plentiful harvest and so much food that no one could number it. But then, the seven years of plenty would be followed by seven years of famine, or in our case, a recession. As a result of the dream, Joseph cautions Pharaoh on what should be done regarding this dilemma that Egypt would soon encounter.

After Joseph assessed the situation, he came up with a plan in which they would store 1/5 or 20% of all the increase during the years of plenty so that in the time of famine, the food would be stored in the store houses to prepare against the seven years of famine. Now you've got to see what's going on here because there is much that we can learn about the current economic recession and the position that God would compose for the Egyptians. God was using a little slave boy to speak to the king regarding the fate of the entire kingdom. Joseph did not have the experience of sitting on the council, nor did he have the influence of power among the rulers of Egypt. For God's sake, he had been in prison!

Joseph was just released from bondage. Yet upon interpreting the dream, he knew exactly what to do because all he had ever done was dream. He knew God had shown him many dreams about his future, so what he did have was experience in knowing what to do with a dream. That's the way it is with many of us. Although we feel like we are currently in bondage to our struggles, God has already shown us a glimpse of where we are going. We have seen it in a dream, and we know that it's God. Admit it... you've seen yourself sitting behind your boss' desk. You have gotten a glimpse of yourself managing the whole operation, or you see yourself speaking to crowds of people in an audience as far as the eye could see. But then, you couldn't see how it was going to happen.

Sometimes you can't see how God is going to snatch you out of your mundane situation where you are bound and frustrated by the same old thing, but you know that one day—all of this will be over, and what God has shown you, will come to pass. You're not gifted for nothing. You're not anointed to just sit in a pit, but in due season, God is going to raise you up to reap the harvest of a realized dream. Frustration causes you to think... God, I'm tired of just seeing it only in my head. You want a change to come because you're bound, and you are sitting there wasting away as a slave to someone else— or worse yet—to your situation. Life can be different, but it doesn't start to happen until you think about what you have seen in your spirit.

Joseph interprets the dream, and what you should notice is his principal instinct was to assess and diagnose the situation. They had a problem, so Joseph sensed that he had to come up with a solution which was the primary step in solving their dilemma. Remember, before we can start recovery, we've got to find and diagnose the problems or the potential obstacles.

So the next thing Joseph did was to formulate a plan. As a result, the people of Egypt went on to enjoy the seven plenteous years following the guidelines of Joseph's plan to store up 1/5 or 20%. This proposal began to look familiar to me as I thought about the process I had used for years in helping my patients to recover. Joseph *assessed* the situation. He then ***diagnosed*** the problem, but then he *planned* for the solution.

The key to solving any real problem involves a process or systematic approach in which there are specific steps that when followed, produce a desired or expected outcome. We can be successful in our approaches if we learn the process of success. It is a problem-solving technique utilized by almost every industry and discipline in the world; and it is as useful in the business world as it is within the medical field or any place in which there is a need or conflict. You may ask— *"Now, what does any of this have to do with the recession or my financial peace?"* There is a very solid correlation, and if you read on, you will soon see how sickness within a patient may be related to any imbalance or battle within your life.

THE PROCESS

While I was going through nursing school, I found some days to be the most difficult times of my life. I was under so much pressure as I tried hard to comprehend the concepts and processes which continually eluded me. All I wanted, at the time, was to learn the material so that I could pass the tests or spew out the correct information upon request from my nursing instructors. I studied feverishly because I really wanted to understand the field, but some areas were just genuinely problematic for me. It's a shame to admit it, but I did not grasp some of the practical steps until after I graduated and started my career.

Have you ever noticed that most problems initially seem insurmountable because they are either so big or complicated, or because we feel so inadequate in the face of the problem? But then one day, you look back on it and realize—that was easy! While you were going through it or right in the midst of it, the problem consumed you so that you could not comprehend the steps you needed to solve it without certain defeat. You felt defeated because you tried to understand the whole picture without breaking it into parts of a process. But that's the only way to deal with a problem. You must participate in the process because the process contains stepping stones to your destiny, and it's half the fun of getting there.

What you learn throughout the process is priceless. During the process, your character is determined. During the process, your gifts are developed, and relationships are cultivated. So you can't fight the process, no matter what you may want to achieve in life. Whether your dream is graduating from college, buying a home, or running a successful business, there is a specific process to it all. Jentezen Franklin wrote in his inspiring book, *Believe That You Can,* "Reaching your dream requires a process—it takes time, persistence, patience." He further points out that living your dreams may not be easy, but asserts that you can do it, and you can even enjoy the process.

Within the following chapters, I will lay out a process or the fundamental steps to recovery. You can use them to deal with any problem from which you want to attain peace. The critical steps resemble the nursing process which is an organized framework used to provide a systematic problem-solving method as it relates to patient care. Stick with me. You don't have to be interested in nursing or the medical field to get this, as I will not digress too far into it. My only intent is to illustrate the basis for setting up an orderly system for you to assess, diagnose, plan, intervene, and evaluate your current situation. Upon doing so, you will emerge more confident and capable of conquering whatever seems to be standing in the way of you and your dreams.

I could say so much more about the process and systems that we encounter and are forced to incorporate on a daily basis, but I believe the most important point to remember is this. While the process may not start out easy, it usually becomes second nature once you understand what's required to handle it. By that, I mean everything gets easier with time and practice. My old nursing school instructor used to say, "Education is just clarification of terms." It took me a while, but I finally realized what he was trying to imply was once I knew what he was talking about, everything else was easy. Once I reduced the components of the concept at hand into simpler terms, I would soon comprehend how to deal with the more complex problem. This process usually started with a simple question or an assessment of the case. Since assessment is the first essential phase in any problem-solving endeavor, we will look to this area as the foundation of our plan for recovery. Our process can only begin if we are diligent in our efforts to start with the assessment of where we are right now and how we can move to where we want to be.

Take this time to think about what has been on your mind lately. What has caused an uneasy feeling in you? We will want to use this information as we start out on the first step of problem-solving, the critical step of assessment.

CHAPTER 3

A TIME FOR ASSESSMENT

A thorough and accurate assessment is the single-most important tool in offering hidden and obvious clues as to what might be causing a given problem. This holds true whether you are assessing mechanical breakdowns in cars, medical deficiencies in patients, or economic dilemmas in America!

In order to begin recovery, we have to launch the process of assessment in a clear and concise manner. This is the time to be specific in your observations and analysis as it is essential in gathering useful information and data which we will use later. In nursing, the assessment would include the patient's current status, a history of the problematic issue and related factors; objective and subjective perceptions of the problem; and the current management of the symptoms.

Here's what you do during your assessment. You must be observant, and get all the facts. In addition to focusing on internal factors, you must also consider external factors which may help or hinder your recovery. Know what's happening in the world around you. What is going on in the market? As you gather all of the important information, you should begin to ask yourself the following:

- What's wrong with the economy?
- What markets are suffering the most?
- Which services or products will still be in demand no matter what?

- Which markets are forced to give concessions in order to stay afloat?

Currently, the economic downturn has sparked a lot of creative and innovative opportunities because the banks have little or no money to lend for important markets like housing and home financing. Right now, investors can buy property directly from the owners who can't get rid of them. Investors can build wealth for much less... and without much of the hassle of a bank or lender as they did in the past. Banks are selling foreclosures as a way to recoup a portion of the money that they will lose due to foreclosures during the recession. I will show you how to obtain the bank's list of foreclosures later in this book. Financial institutions are also paying more interest on products like certificates of deposit (commonly referred to as "CDs"), because they need the money right now. Can you see the apparent transference of wealth about to take place, and the recession is a great tool to usher it into the lives of those who seek after it.

So you've got to assess what's going on around you and ascertain how it affects you and your goals of getting better. In addition to observing you surroundings, your assessment should include an introspective look at you so that you may get rid of all the denial and see yourself as you really are. Ask questions like:

- What are the obvious areas that I need to change?
- What are the obstacles blocking me from getting where I really want to be?
- What small step can I take to get closer to my goal?

But then, don't forget to ask yourself:

- What's right with me?
- What gifts can I develop to help others?
- What do I have to offer right now?

You can still prosper in the midst of a recession if you are sensitive to the external factors and decide to use them to your advantage. Don't tell me it can't happen. Madam C. J. Walker became the first African-American, female millionaire almost a century ago when the country was on the brink of the great depression of the 1930's. Her family continues to enjoy the benefits of her labor and her drive to succeed in the face of adversity. She saw a need within an industry and realized that women were willing to pay in order to maintain their beauty—no matter what.

Bill Gates, one of the most influential people in the world, reportedly started Microsoft during the turbulent financial times of 1975 and the oil bust which would ensue in the early 1980's. As documented in his biographical profile, here's how he revolutionized the technological world:

> "Bill Gates started studying at Harvard University in 1973 where he spent time with Paul Allen. Gates and Allen worked on a version of the programming language BASIC. That was the basis for the MITS Altair (the first microcomputer available). He did not go on to graduate from Harvard University as he left in his junior year to start what was to become the largest computer software company in the world; Microsoft Corporation." (http://www.woopidoo.com/biography/bill-gates.htm).

Imagine how difficult it must have been to follow his dream and face his parents to explain why he was dropping out of college in his junior year. They must have been elated to learn that all of the time and money they spent was going to be used by this 20 year old venturing off into something no one had dared to try before. He undoubtedly made a decision to proceed after assessing his own goals and believing in his strength to achieve them.

IDENTIFY YOUR STRENGTHS

Identifying where you are and recognizing your strengths (and weaknesses) will aid you in advancing toward your ultimate dream. Once you have done this, you will be able to formulate a useful plan that will cancel out the fear and powerlessness you may feel now or the fear others attempt to deposit within you. Author and motivational speaker, Chris Gardner declares in his book, *Start Where You Are*, "...If you're ready to part ways with feeling hopeless or fearful, there are possibilities to be pursued that you may not have considered." Allow me to reiterate, there is always hope as long as there is breath in your body.

Once all of the assessment information is collected and the checklist is complete, the process is then set into motion with the organized data. Specific indicators are singled out, and the diagnosis, or the basis for the diagnosis, is given. Now it's time for the plan of action to be formulated and presented as a care plan or prescription for treatment. The preliminary diagram of a simple plan of care may resemble the following chart:

ASSESSMENT	DIAGNOSIS
-Excessive Debt & Financial Obligations -Loss of job/income -Limited skills/experience	-Alteration in Financial Peace -Fear of Bankruptcy -Fear of Homelessness -Powerlessness

In performing your assessment, you should also take a specific account of where you are financially. Getting out of debt requires that you first know where you are and how much you currently owe. How much income your receive in relation to how much you spend each month are also key factors to getting out of debt faster. Remember to be specific so that you may ask for the exact amount you require to pay it all off. Also provided for you in this chapter are sample worksheets and tables to help you organize yourself and assess where you are.

Worksheet 1
Current Debts

Current Debts	Current Balance	Minimum Monthly Payment	# of Months to Pay Off
Credit Card #1	$1,500.00	$150.00	10
Car Note	$12,000.00	$763.18	15
Credit Card #2	$4,884.00	$125.00	39
Student Loans	$5,900.00	$116.95	50
Credit Card #3	$4,931.04	$90.00	55
Installment Loan	$7,800.00	$125.00	62
Mortgage #1	$273,000.00	$2,602.00	105
Total Debt	**$374,182.04**	**$4,464.13**	

You will notice that we added a column titled "# of Months to Pay Off". This column is critical as it will be your indicator for selecting the debt/creditor you will attack first. Once you have listed all of your current debts, current balances, and minimum monthly payment amounts, you can figure the number of months to pay off a debtor by using the following formula:

Current Balance / Monthly Payment = # of Months to Pay Off
Example: $1,500.00/$150.00= 10 months

Using our example, you see that it will take 10 months to pay off your first debt of $1,500.00. You should attack this debt using the $150 minimum payment and any additional amount you can add to pay this debt off first. If you can add just another $25 extra to this payment, then you can retire the debt faster and free yourself of this payment in 8.5 months. Once you are done with Debt #1, add the entire amount ($150 + $25) to the next debt on the list. This will help you to pay out Debt #2 in less than the 15 months allotted, and so on. If you are disciplined enough to stay focused on this plan, you will be financially free in no time.

Most financial strategists will tell you to pay off your smallest balance first, and that would be effective on your quest to financial freedom, but if you are paying $30 a month on a $1,000 balance, it would take you 33 months or longer to pay off this balance. However, if you apply the first strategy (attacking the balance with the least amount of months to pay off), you would make larger, progressive steps toward your goals more rapidly. You would experience such a sense of accomplishment in a shorter period of time, and that would invigorate you to continue. There is certainly more than one way to achieve any given goal, but I say work smarter, not harder. This chapter will help you to assess what you have, and you will decide the best way to use it.

Worksheet 2
Monthly Budget

INCOME SOURCES	SOURCE	AMOUNT
Monthly Income Source #1:		
Monthly Income Source #2:		
Monthly Income Source #3:		
Monthly Income Source #4:		
Total Income		
MONTHLY EXPENSES	**AMOUNT BUDGETED**	**AMOUNT SPENT**
Charitable Giving		
Church/Religious Organizations		
Other		
Other		
Savings		
IRA/Retirement Accounts		
Money Market/Savings Accounts		
Emergency Fund		
Other		
Total Savings		
Housing		
Mortgage/Rent		
Property taxes		
Homeowner's/Renter's Insurance		

MONTHLY EXPENSES	AMOUNT BUDGETED	AMOUNT SPENT
Electric		
Gas		
Water/Sewerage		
Other utilities		
Lawn Care		
Cleaning		
Maintenance/Repairs		
Alarm System		
Telephone		
Cell Phone		
Other		
Total Housing:		
Automobile		
Auto Payment #1		
Auto Payment #2		
Gas Auto #1		
Gas Auto #2		
Maintenance/Repair		
Auto detailing		
Parking		
Public transportation		
Other		
Total Auto		

MONTHLY EXPENSES	AMOUNT BUDGETED	AMOUNT SPENT
Food		
Groceries		
Lunch/Meals at work		
Snacks		
Kids' lunches		
Fast food		
Meals out		
Coffee/Beverages		
Other		
Total Food		
Education/Child Care		
Tuition		
Day Care		
After Care		
Books		
Supplies		
Baby-sitting		
Summer Camp		
Allowance		
Extracurricular Activities		
Other		
Total Education/Childcare		

MONTHLY EXPENSES	AMOUNT BUDGETED	AMOUNT SPENT
Health		
Insurance premiums		
Doctor visits/co-pays		
Prescription medicine		
Over-the-counter meds		
Supplements		
Medical supplies		
Vision(co-pays, glasses/ contacts		
Other		
Total Health		
Entertainment		
Movies/Concerts		
Movie rentals		
Cable TV		
Internet service		
Sporting Events		
Books		
Magazine subscriptions		
CDs/Music		
Birthday/Holiday parties		
Gifts		
Other		
Total Entertainment		

MONTHLY EXPENSES	AMOUNT BUDGETED	AMOUNT SPENT
Insurance		
Disability		
Life		
Credit		
Auto		
Extended Warranty		
Other		
Total Insurance		
Pets		
Food		
Medical		
Supplies		
Grooming		
Other		
Total Pets		
Clothing		
Professional attire		
Leisure attire		
Hosiery/Socks		
Underwear/Lingerie		
Shoes/Accessories		
Jewelry		
Dry Cleaning		
Other		
Total Clothing		

MONTHLY EXPENSES	AMOUNT BUDGETED	AMOUNT SPENT
Personal Care		
Haircuts/Perms/Coloring		
Manicure/Pedicure/Waxing		
Gym Membership		
Other		
Vacation		
Airfare/Gas		
Auto Rentals		
Lodging		
Food		
Souvenirs		
Baggage Fees		
Other		
Total Vacation		
Holidays		
Gifts		
Decorating		
Entertainment		
Other		
Total Holidays		
TOTAL MONTHLY EXPENSES		

*Resource adapted from *The ABC's of Getting Out of Debt*

CHAPTER 4

A TIME FOR DIAGNOSIS

Ask any health care worker, and they will tell you that *"early diagnosis usually offers the best prognosis"* meaning—the sooner your problem is identified, the more options and available treatments there will be to correct or alleviate the problem. While this may be true, some of us continue to prolong assessment and diagnosis because we simply do not want to face the truth. It is typically never a good time to get a diagnosis of cancer. No matter the diagnosis, the patient understands that there will be changes and alterations to our lifestyle if we desire to control the disease process.

You will notice that I use the collective terms, "us" and "we" in this segment. Well, here's the reason. As I write this chapter, I am attempting to incorporate the recent adaptations I have faced since being diagnosed with Type 2 Diabetes Mellitus. I cannot begin to explain the drop in my spirit the day my doctor's office contacted me with the news. I was on the road traveling back from our family vacation when the medical assistant called to advise me that the doctor wanted me to return for a follow up visit and evaluation. She suspected I had Diabetes since my family history was positive for the disease and my recent blood test results were abnormally high. I drove on in disbelief refusing to mention the content of my conversation in the presence of my children.

The remainder of the road trip was extremely somber to say the least. It was all I could do to keep the tears from streaming down as

I heard myself on many occasions declare...."It will never happen to me." I prided myself on eating right, staying fit, and I believed that I would escape the disease I dreaded so much as I had seen firsthand the effects and complications caused by this common disease process. According to the American Diabetes Association, "Type 2 diabetes is the most common form of diabetes. Millions of Americans have been diagnosed with type 2 diabetes, and many more are unaware they are at high risk." (http://www.diabetes.org/diabetes-basics/type-2). I could not believe it! How could this be happening to me?

After a brief period of shock and awe, I resolved on a way to deal with the news. I would ignore it. I would continue to eat healthy and exercise as I knew the usual prescribed diet and treatment regimen for diabetic patients. I didn't need a physician to tell me or prescribe any insulin shots for me. So why should I have returned to see her? After all, I would get this under control and see her later during my annual visits. Was I in denial or what? I chose to bury my head in the sand and ignore further signs and symptoms that something was indeed wrong. The events that occurred next were enough to pull me out of my stupor.

DIAGNOSIS CONFIRMED

Approximately one month following my refusal to return to the doctor's office, I was stung twice by a bee and forced to go to the emergency room for treatment because of extreme swelling, itching, and pain to the affected leg. Upon my initial assessment, the nurse measured my vital signs and assessed my blood sugar level. What did my blood sugar level have to do with anything? It was just a bee sting. Well, what I was soon told by the emergency room physician was this... the affected area had delayed healing because my blood sugar level was elevated which caused inadequate blood perfusion to the leg. My level was 238, an abnormal value considering the normal range of 80-125 mg/dl. The physician then ordered that I return to my primary care physician for further evaluation and treatment. When I returned, additional tests showed abnormally high levels which confirmed a diagnosis of diabetes.

I was dismayed to hear her say the words, and I sat there as if in a movie scene as I watched her load of all the diabetic supplies into a little brown bag. She then said to me something that was very liberating. Her words of encouragement were… "The diagnosis may be bad news for you, but it's not the end of your life. You can control the disease with diet and exercise, so I will not prescribe any medicines for you now." Why was this so liberating? Well, she had just given me two weapons to fight and control my own destiny. After I regrouped and looked at the situation differently, I would be able to handle anything that came along. I had been meaning to make a few lifestyle changes anyway. Now, I would definitely have the discipline to exercise and watch what I ate in order to control the disease.

In a matter of months, I began to noticed marked weight loss (a desired effect of dieting), and soon I began to realize that maybe this wasn't such a bad thing after all. What I kept putting off for a later time in life was thrust upon me suddenly, but it was the best time to start a life-altering change. I was just about to hit my 40's, and as far as I was concerned, life was just beginning! My student loans were just about paid off, I had purchased the home I always wanted, and I was enjoying a wonderful, prosperous career. I wasn't about to allow a diagnosis to stop me. I feel better than I have ever felt in my life.

IT'S A DIAGNOSIS, NOT A DEATH SENTENCE

A diagnosis, by definition, is the identification or conclusion of a matter after careful analysis. The diagnosis places a label on the notions or observations that are discovered during the assessment. It is not always easy to discover and accurately label a diagnosis even though we have clear and concise assessment information.

For instance, the television drama, *House MD* is one of my favorite shows. During most episodes, the clinical team goes through many different diagnoses because they address the symptoms of what is primarily evident in the patient. But the diagnosis is usually ruled out as the patient exhibits additional symptoms, and the team is forced to go back to the drawing board and attempt to get a more accurate assessment to later arrive at the true and precise diagnosis.

While everyone would like to place an exact diagnosis on the disaster that resulted from the American financial meltdown of our present economic system, I think Chris Gardner put it best: "With a wonton disregard for consequences, Wall Street perpetuated the "HIV of finance" that has now infected the central nervous system of the global economy." This is an unfortunate diagnosis, but it's not a death sentence. We still have to live and operate within this economy, and the good news is we can not only recover, but we can thrive.

Prior to receiving the diagnosis of diabetes, I could not explain the periods of fatigue and other symptoms I experienced. It wasn't until further assessment and intense research that I was able to be informed of the diagnosis, and sometimes this is what needs to happen with our financial situations. If you want to experience financial wellness, you must research and discover the diagnosis before you can plan to prevent the undesired effects in your life.

How can you prevent a lack of finances and debt struggles all the time? Look at your diagnosis of over-spending, and see what plan you can devise to correct the problem. Are you spending so much in the wrong areas that you don't have enough to really invest in things that will bring you a return? Make a plan to cut back in your over-indulgent areas to save for good investments.

CHAPTER 5

A TIME FOR PLANNING

The planning phase is the period of preparation or a time designated to write out and develop a strategy to repair the problems you have identified. This is the measure wherein you develop specific guidelines to gauge your goals. You specify exact numbers and express definite, detailed terms instead of vague requests.

Shortly after taking time off from the medical field, my passion for purchasing investment property led me to study real estate and acquire a real estate license so that I might develop greater skills in buying, selling, and negotiating. I also wanted to assist others in meeting their financial goals through real estate investing and realizing the dream of homeownership. I must say, that the industry is an interesting field not much different from nursing in that I meet so many people who are all striving to get better. My real estate clients usually admit to me that they are attempting to purchase a specific property because they want a better place to live; or they want to improve their quality of life with a better home, money, and security for the future.

As a real estate sales associate, I operate under the direction of a broker whose main objective, among other supervisory functions, is to motivate and encourage me to be the best real estate sales associate I can be. In so doing, we often attend sales and motivational meetings in which we plan for success in sales by setting goals to achieve what we want out of life. One day, shortly after starting in real estate, my broker challenged us to carry out goal-setting sessions. This exercise was a written checklist which contained various areas that would be assessed on a scale of 1-10 with 1 being the weakest and 10 being the strongest values of measure. The indicators included areas such as the financial, spiritual, physical, relational, educational, and career aspects of our lives.

In addition to this exercise, he also had us to write down our goals for each major area, but he swiftly admonished us to set a measurable goal and attach a specific date or time frame of when we would have the goal met. Year after year, I would spend quality time thinking of the goals I wanted to achieve for the year, and I would diligently write them down with specific dates and all. I would then visualize my goals, as often as I could, while also speaking some of them aloud.

I loved this goal-setting technique because; of course I had previous nursing experience with the effectiveness of goal-setting. I knew the power of assessing, collecting, and organizing information in attempts to compile a plan of action. You may have noticed that I performed all of the key functions that are taught by the best motivational coaches in the world. All of them will advise you on the secrets of getting what you want and fulfilling your desires by first writing and visualizing your goals. Does it work? Yes, it does—to some degree. But I could not help but notice that at the end of every year; only a small portion of my goals had been achieved while the majority of them went unrealized. Although they were specifically written with dates and time frames attached, they didn't come to fruition in the time I had set. I also fervently visualized them and saw myself achieving each and every one of them, but still—only a small percentage of my goals materialized.

What was I doing wrong? Why wasn't this plan working for me? Well, I believe that all of the goal-setting steps were essential. They helped me to get clear on what I wanted, and writing of the dreams and goals caused me to organize my thoughts. But there was something missing. The exercises alone were not effective for me because I had goals with no corresponding actions. Allow me to explain.

THE PLAN WON'T WORK UNTIL YOU WORK THE PLAN

While I was completing the written exercises and formulating the checklist, I was not acting upon the plan. It is the same scenario as if you were to go to the physician's office for a check up. The doctor would examine you, write down all of your symptoms, but then send you home with nothing. No plan to help you recover... no prescriptions to fight the disease or symptoms... and no information to assist you in understanding what's going wrong in your body. A thorough and complete check up involves a physical examination, as well as, an observation of your medical history. Certain questions evolve, and the medical staff may ask questions like: How long have you been experiencing the problem? What are your complaints at this time? Who else in your family has experienced the same problems? These are just a few of the questions that may arise during your assessment; but they are all pertinent, and they will assist in the diagnosis and treatment of your issue.

When you collect the information, be prepared to also implement a plan. Use the tools you have collected and give attention to the plan you have designed in order to expect the desired results. You can **not** just write the plan or the goals, but you have to work the plan. No matter how detailed you are in your planning, you must get up and act upon what you have written, or YOU GET NOTHING. This was the missing link for me... The secret to why I was not getting the most out of these goal-setting sessions.

THE SECRET TO SUCCESS

The secret to success and reaping abundance isn't much different from the secret to fulfilling any of life's goals. There is a process that most successful people use, and it gives them a huge, competitive advantage over most. They understand the difference between "goal-setting" and "goal-getting". While they utilize all of the conventional methods of writing, visualizing, and measuring goals, they understand the importance of an oft forgotten aspect of getting what you want. I'll share with you how to formulate your plan and find the missing link of your success. When you formulate your plan, you begin to jump start your success, and there is nothing that you can't achieve. As I stated earlier, it all starts with an assessment, and the following steps helped me to move from *writing* to *winning!*

One day, as I reviewed my goal checklist, I asked myself an important question about the goals I had written. What am I doing to achieve these goals? Suddenly, I realized that I hadn't given much thought to the necessary steps to move me closer to attaining my goals. What did I intend to do to achieve even the smallest step toward getting what I listed? At that point, I remembered the process, and suddenly I knew why I had spent thousands of dollars and countless hours in nursing school. It was all to learn the process of solving critical problems and achieving goals.

Don't just write your goals at the beginning of the year without a commitment to do what you said you would do. Many of us know what to do in order to improve our unwanted conditions, but the problem is just doing it. Nobody said it was going to be easy, but if we are going to get to our place of promise where there are rewards and reaping, it's going to be a process, and it's going to take a little sacrifice.

No matter how accurate and complete the assessment or diagnosis, none of it will be of use, and it will all be ineffective, if the plan is never implemented and followed. Consider the following example.

Every year, my dear friend hires a personnel trainer to help him lose weight. Like most of us, he is very committed in the first few months of the year as he meets with the trainer to compile a personalized weight loss plan with exercises, nutritional components, and behavioral modifications included. Needless to say, that all of this is very time consuming and expensive, but it's the necessary steps that he must take in order to realize his goal of weight loss. So the plan is customized with all of the data such as his specific body mass index, his age, height, base heart rate, etc. His daily exercise schedules and meal regimens are set. He visualizes himself as a size 34. He even says it as he reviews the plan constantly, but there is something missing. He never implements the plan or puts forth any consistent effort to realize his goal. Does he really want to drop the weight? Of course he does. Does he think that it can really happen? Of course it can. But it will never happen until he acts upon what he knows and what he sees in his head. Allow me to repeat…you **cannot** just write the plan or the goals, but you have to work the plan. No matter how detailed you are in your planning, you must get up and act upon what you have written, or YOU GET NOTHING.

I know that sometimes life can leave you crushed and crippled, but you either make the decision to get the help you need to recover, or you die with unfulfilled plans and dreams. If you stay in your present situation, then death is certain, but if you face the unknown and move out past your fears, who knows what you can achieve. So you may not be able to do it alone. You may not be able to handle all that life is throwing at you right now as your plans seem to crumble and fail.

Well, I think if you utilize the right steps by assessing and diagnosing your situation, you can set your plan with specific goals into action. But remember to consider your intentions to develop steps you are willing to take in order to achieve your desired results. Connect with someone who can strengthen you when you don't know exactly how to get what you want.

CHAPTER 6

A TIME FOR INTERVENTION

An intervention may be described in terms of interference or forced interruption of the problematic, destructive behavior of another. Most commonly seen upon a family member or friend intervening in the case of a substance abuser, the intervener understands that the suffering subject is helpless in the face of whatever has them bound. Whether an addiction to drugs, alcohol, or any other type of abusive conduct, someone has to make the sacrifice to act on behalf of the substance user. As an act of love, they reach out as they have finally made a decision to "do something" to stop the destruction. Only unconditional love and a willingness to save the subject's life will motivate the intervener to provide support and initiate gradual change or immediate cessation of the habitual activity.

According to The Partnership for a Drug-Free America, "The point of any intervention is to ask the person to take concrete steps to address the problem and lead them to the help they need." (http://www.drugfree.org).

Now before you start to judge or think about that "other person" who may be addicted or bound by something, I implore you to think about your addiction. What addiction? So maybe it's not drugs, alcohol, or gambling; but most of us have a self-defeating behavior or habit which may be causing us the problems that plague us.

57

Simply put, we all have something over which we should exert a little more control. What about the excessive spending or those of us who spend just as much in the mall as the gambler spends in the casino. If you can't say "amen"— say "ouch!" I know I may have stepped on your toes a little with that observation. Why is it so hard to change even when we know we have a problem that's out of control? What does it take to admit we have a problem so that we can get the help we need?

While it is true that most of us would like to believe we are in control of every situation, it is certain that there are times when we feel like our circumstances are spinning out of control, and we are unable to defend ourselves in the face of difficult challenges and external forces. After struggling and fighting for such a long time without the desired results, we often feel like throwing up our hands in surrender. Have you ever tried to keep it all together; but nothing seemed to help, so you determined... "What's the use?" Do you ever have the thought of giving up? It's only natural to feel so depleted inside as the things that worked in the past are no longer working for your current issue. You feel as though you are in bondage, and it seems that no prayer and no formula of faith will do it for this crisis.

WHAT DO YOU DO WHEN YOU DON'T KNOW WHAT TO DO?

What do you do when you don't know what to do concerning your problems? Although it may seem futile to ask, I often find myself pondering similar questions when I feel totally helpless and powerless against a situation or crisis. The pressure of revealed failure is the biggest fear, so the initial reaction is to paint the picture as though everything is under control. But what happens when it starts to totally fall apart? Your private struggles begin to leak into your public sectors, and you have the urge to make something happen.

What you will soon discover is you are in the same place of uncertainty where most of us eventually arrive, at least for a certain season in our lives. As the effects of the recession rip on, so many of us feel helpless now that the savings are gone, all the reserves are depleted, and the world systems are constantly changing. Although we tried to do it according to the plan, we are still facing setbacks and circumstances that cause us stress and worry. You have to ask yourself the question... How did you get to this point?

HOW DID WE GET HERE?

So how did we end up in this place of dependence and subjection to forces outside of our control? Why do we need to depend on others to get out of this mess? Who can help you out of your desperate situation? As difficult as it may seem, we have to find a way to break free of the bondage and internal frustrations we are currently experiencing. It's the only way to push pass the feelings of powerlessness, loneliness, and helplessness. If you can identify with any of these feelings, then you are in a true battle; but there is something you must stop to do as you attempt to get better. That is what this chapter is all about. It's about stopping to come to your senses and to admit that you need an intervention. The load is too heavy, and you are not equipped to continue carrying it alone.

One of the most liberating things in life is the freedom that comes from admitting that maybe you can't handle it! You need the assistance of another to fight against what perplexes you— someone to help you recover. You must realize that you are not in this alone. The enemy would love nothing more than to engage you in a fight causing you to believe that you must fight all by yourself. We are already defeated if we think we will be able to overcome any real fight in our own strength, with our own weapons, and without the assistance of others. You have heard it said, "Everybody needs somebody sometimes." Well, it is totally true. We are sure to win when we are fortified by the strength of others who have our best interest at heart.

You should know that you are not surrendering or giving up in weakness when you realize that you need help. In fact, it at this point when you are at your strongest as you are taking the first, legitimate step toward recovery. Even the greatest world leaders and the most noble of rulers can only conquer when they are resourceful enough to harness the experience and expertise of those who are useful to them.

From time to time, we all have periods of grief and experiences of desolation. This is the time when we need the support of someone else to see us through. Additionally, it truly helps to solicit the testimony of someone with whom you can identify in the moment of crisis. That's the reason why recovering substance abusers fair best when they are assisted by an individual who has "been there before" and beat the odds. They can attest to the bondage and particular struggle the person feels, and they know exactly what steps are necessary to get out.

Usually, the connections that we assemble cause us to excel and achieve the goals we desire—no matter how great or small. Once we admit there is a problem which we cannot overcome alone, an intervener will emerge and help us through to recovery.

I NEED AN INTERVENTION!

There comes a time when God wants to prove to us that we are not self-sufficient. We did not hold everything together and create the desired results on our own in the past, so why not depend on Him for the help we need now? I'll tell you why. It's usually a struggle of a different kind. It's called PRIDE with a capital "P". We need an intervention, but we are afraid to admit it because we are taught to be self-sufficient and to carry our own load. Many would rather lose it all and even face death rather than reach out and ask for help. You may think this sounds extreme, but it's certainly true. We have a difficult time asking for assistance and admitting we have somehow made the wrong decisions and failed in a certain area.

Pride has caused us to mask our mistakes and to continue pretending as though everything is good as we go on in denial about our circumstances. My prayer is that you will not continue in such a state. This great recession is the perfect time to resist all egotism and admit it. We made the wrong decisions, and many of us are suffering as a result of the economic downturn. We messed up, and we can not fix it on our on. We don't have all the answers for the peace that continually eludes us. World-renowned evangelist, Billy Graham stated, "All people are seeking the answer to the confusion, the moral sickness, the spiritual emptiness that oppresses the world. We are all crying out for guidance, for comfort, for happiness, for peace."

America, in all of its superiority and patriotism portrays the symbol that epitomizes pride and promotes the climate for self-reliance. While this is admirable in some regards, it often prevents accordance and stifles the unity required for change. For instance, as consumers and businesses continue to focus on survival and economic recovery, the greater challenge will be getting the political and special interest groups on the same page. No one wants to admit that we made mistakes, and now we need help. The feds still believe that we can lower interest rates and cut taxes to increase consumption and ignite recovery, but that only provides a band-aid for a deeper, more gaping wound.

Although it's too soon to judge whether all of the proposed bills and stimulus packages will prove to be great investments, it's pleasing to know that help is on the way. A recently published Newsweek article entitled, *The Recession is Over,* indicated that "the Obama administration's strategy rests on what some might call industrial policy or excessive government intervention." The article admits that we need a new kind of recovery, and I couldn't agree more. We need interventions to help us in our recovery, and while government interventions may be useful; they are definitely not sufficient all alone. If we are to survive our uncertain times and personal struggles, we have got to participate in this recovery.

So as you come to admit the need for an intervention for your situation, you will come to appreciate another concept called "intercession", for the two are somewhat synonymous. Like an intervention, intercession is effective due to the interference of another. Intercession is the act of mediation or standing between two parties.

THE HOLY SPIRIT IS AN INTERCESSOR

God declares that the Holy Spirit is our intercessor. Romans 8:26-28 says this:

Likewise the Spirit also helps in our weaknesses. For we do not know what we should pray for as we ought, but the Spirit Himself makes intercession for us with groanings which cannot be uttered. Now He who searches the hearts knows what the mind of the Spirit is, because He makes intercession for the saints according to the will of God.

And we know that all things work together for good to those who love God, to those who are the called according to His purpose.

New King James Version

It is good news to know that although we don't know what to say, what to think, or what to do—there is someone who does. The Holy Spirit is there to comfort and keep us when it seems like all hell is breaking loose in our lives. Not too long ago, I needed the comfort of the Holy Spirit. I needed to remember all of the promises of God during a very discouraging and uncertain hour in my life, and I am glad to report that he kept me. The Holy Spirit kept my mind, and he kept my heart. The power of a still, small voice encouraged me when I felt like giving up. That was a true intervention, but the Holy Spirit does not work alone. Jesus is also an intercessor for all who will allow him to help in our recovery.

JESUS IS AN INTERCESSOR

He saw that there was no man, and wondered that there was no intercessor; Therefore His own arm brought salvation for Him; and His own righteousness, it sustained Him.

For He put on righteousness as a breastplate, and a helmet of salvation on His head; He put on the garments of vengeance for clothing, and was clad with zeal as a cloak.

Isaiah 59:16-17 — New King James Version

The preceding verses describe the condition of the earth as God looked down and saw man, in his sinful state, as disconnected from His presence. He needed a way to redeem man and bring him out of darkness back into the light of truth. When He could find no man worthy, He decided to come, in the form of man as the Lord,

Jesus Christ. Jesus is the intercessor who continually mediates for us through all of our mistakes; He redeems us and causes us to rise above whatever has us bound. Talk about a recovery! We all need that intervention to live a life of joy and the peace that surpasses all understanding.

A WORD ABOUT INTERVENTIONS

Interventions are integral factors in attaining goals, and each goal should have at least one corresponding intervention. In other words, goals are only achieved with active involvement of the subject and scrutiny on the part of the one who sets the goal. Think if you will, of a patient who needs to recover from recent surgery. There are all types of measures that must be performed in order for recovery to be expedient. Most times, there is a specific protocol of interventions in the first few hours after surgery, and they include various functions by the nurse; but all are performed with the goals in mind. For instance, assessment of vital signs would be foremost in monitoring the patient's stability. Secondly, the prescribed medicine or treatments would be rendered. Well, you get the picture. The nurse must provide the crucial, necessary actions to a powerless being in efforts to meet the goal of recovery.

Your interventions to recovery will be similar to these steps in that they are vital steps formulated in response to the set goals. As a part of the plan, this segment will give life and purpose to your aspirations. Assessment is asking, "Where am I now", but interventions ask, "What can I do to get where I want to be." It means inquiring about the steps to take to achieve what you want.

So what do you want to achieve? Write it down as a goal, and add the corresponding interventions you will perform on the side of it. What do you intend to do in order to get one step closer to achieving what you desire most? Intentions, like goals are stated in specific amounts and other measurements set for your life; but intentions allow for more than the confines of the set boundaries we set with our finite minds. Intentions always allow for the "something greater" or measures that far exceed our expectations.

In an instance, I added the steps I would take toward measures I was willing to implement in order to achieve my stated goals. Here's how it works. If I wrote a goal as follows:

By the 31ˢᵗ day of December 2009, I will have at least 580,000.00 or more in net worth...

I would add to it: *What do I intend to do to achieve this goal?*
1) *Provide quality customer service to all clients in efforts to gain referrals and increase opportunities*
2) *Earn extra commissions and bonuses to save more*
3) *Locate and read resource material on how others have increased their net worth*

These are my intentions, and they empower me to push toward achieving my goals. They also cause me to constantly focus on where I am on the continuum of attaining the goal. Once you have thought about and formulated your intentions, your plan of recovery should start to develop accordingly:

ASSESSMENT	DIAGNOSIS	PLAN/GOALS	INTERVENTIONS
Excessive Debt & Financial Obligations	Alteration in Financial Peace	Generate enough income to eliminate debt and save for financial emergencies	Sell assets, get part-time job, garage sale, etc. to obtain extra funds
Loss of job/ income	Fear of Bankruptcy	Pay off at least 2 credit cards by 12/31/10	Set a budget and alter spending habits to reduce monthly expenses
Limited skills/ experience	Powerlessness	Regain financial independence and control of finances	Call creditors to ask for special payment arrangements Seek/Obtain information on financial resources and credit counseling Increase skills and Knowledge in area of interest

The table offers a flow sheet which readily organizes your thoughts and clearly provides clues to the etiology and causes of your specific problems (diagnoses). As such, you should be able to derive solutions as you formulate interventions to counteract the issues you detect about yourself. For instance, if you assess that you are unhappy in all of your personal relationships, your diagnosis may be: "Alteration in peace or contentment in relationships". Your plan or goals would include measures to find happier, healthier relationships with people whom you enjoy and have mutual interests.

Remember interventions ask… What can I do to get what I want or where I want to be? Therefore, the next step would entail formulating intentions or interventions to help you get the results you desire. Interventions that come to mind include:

1) **Visiting places of your interests.**
   If you love reading, then you should try hanging out at the bookstore or your local coffee house. There are many avid readers there.

2) **Communicate your feelings of distress to those with whom you share an unhappy relationship.**
   Many times, the stressors we experience come from holding in or suppressing negative feelings. They may not be receptive to your emotional perception of the relationship, but if you are tactful and sincere in your approach, you will have taken the best steps toward freeing yourself. They will understand it better later on, but for now... it's about what you need to achieve your goals and desires.

3) **Do something that makes you happy alone.**
   No matter how much we like to be with other people or be there for others, we must first learn to be happy with us. Doing something on your own that makes you happy is finding an activity or place that gives you joy apart from everything else. Recovery involves experiencing that which is therapeutic. So if you gain pleasure sitting on a park bench soaking up the sun, do that. Set an intention to go to the location at least 15 minutes a week. Your recovery depends upon your ability to participate in your plan of care, and you must take care of you in order to reach your goals.

CHAPTER 7

A TIME FOR EVALUATION

By now, you should be aware of the major components of formulating a plan to conquer any problem that's standing in the way of you and your desires. Now it's time to evaluate your progress on the plan so far. This process is a journey, but you will soon see that it's not a long, linear journey. By contrast, it is a systematic, cyclical journey which causes you to start again with another type of assessment called "evaluation".

If you have made it through the prerequisite steps, you will eventually come to evaluation, the closing stage of the process. While this phase may be regarded as the last, it is not the end of the process but rather a commencement as this segment calls upon you to stop and assess your actions and interventions thus far to see how much progress you have made. Are you effective in your actions? Does your plan work for you? Are you any closer to your goals than you were a year ago?

It is important to point out here that evaluations are also both subjective and objective as you will use predetermined indicators to confirm the success of your plan. You know where you are and where you want to be. You know how much you have really accomplished, so you should be honest with yourself; and make the adjustments to your plan if necessary. You will start by reviewing your goals and corresponding interventions again. See which interventions were useful in accomplishing your objectives and which ones

67

were not. If they did not work, get rid of them and develop new strategies to implement. This measure keeps you in a constant state of self-evaluation in which you assess yourself and your level of peace, for only *you* can appraise the real value of that.

In nursing, there is a specific saying about pain... "Pain is whatever the patient says it is." Of course there are various types of charts and pain-rating scales that range from facial drawings (for those who can not verbally respond to the caregiver regarding pain), to numerical scales rating pain from 0-10 with 10 being the worst possible pain experience. But when it really comes down to it, no one can really know your internal feelings of pain because each person experiences and copes with pain in a unique way. Comparatively, success is similar to this pain concept. No one can impose their concept of success or failure upon you. Realization of success for you may be entirely different from my level or notion of success. That's the reason why it is subjective. It is what you say it is, and it's where you find contentment.

I used to think everyone wanted to excel at their jobs enough so as to eventually get to upper level management and run the entire business. That was the definition of success for me, but then that was for me. I also thought that everyone shared my view of the American dream... to buy a home, get a great job (making at least $100,000 per year), have 2 children, drive the latest model car of my choosing... well you get the picture. I later realized, after making all the financial mistakes and evaluating my financial situation, that it wasn't the definition of success— not even for me. In time, I would come to appreciate the reality that people achieve success on different levels, and what they accomplish in their specific arenas could very well be the wealth that they seek. My definition of success is presently defined in terms of peace— peace in my body, peace in my relationships, and peace within my finances.

By anyone's estimation, Mother Theresa was a huge success in reaching her life's calling because she is regarded by most as the greatest humanitarian who ever lived. Her selfless acts of mercy and care for the poverty-stricken people of her country propelled her to act and change the conditions of many for the greater good of her community. Although she was not rich in regards to personal or material wealth, the impact she made on the lives of all who met her is invaluable. The contributions she made undoubtedly granted the personal satisfaction and fulfillment she sought. Many people were drawn to her quiet strength and were often compelled to visit her to merely observe the secret of her success. What Mother Theresa possessed was the success of knowing peace and the courage of going after her calling. Because her strength emanated from within, it didn't matter that her surroundings were stricken with poverty and turmoil. What made her great was her ability to convey the peace and mercy of God. Although her impact was enormous and felt throughout the world, it contrasted her petite stature and the little acts of kindness that made her a great legend.

So what about your strengths? Which *'little'* attributes do you have that make you the best at what you do and make you feel successful no matter your surroundings? These are thought-provoking questions that continue to stimulate your thinking and take you on a journey of exploration into "you". That's what I believe is the best thing about this recession—time to explore "you" and evaluate the possibilities of what you are and what you may become. Take a *recess* during the recession to discover the best part about you. Many thriving companies have done the same during turbulent economic times.

Occasionally, businesses subject themselves to a SWOT analysis in which they evaluate their *strengths, weaknesses, opportunities,* and *threats.* According to Wikipedia.com, a SWOT Analysis "involves specifying the objective of the business venture or project and identifying the internal and external factors that are favorable and unfavorable to achieving that objective." Fortune 500 companies use these strategic plans developed by Stanford University professor, Albert Humphrey to understand how they might strengthen their corporate structures and continue to profit in an ever-evolving atmosphere and in times of economic distress. Although they have proven useful in the corporate world, I have found this type of technique to be helpful in evaluating personal strengths, weaknesses, opportunities, and threats.

SWOT ANALYSIS

	Helpful to achieving the objective	Harmful to achieving the objective
Internal origin (attributes of the organization)	Strengths	Weaknesses
External origin (attributes of the environment)	Opportunities	Threats

Diagram, as adapted from File: SWOT en.svg, is an illustration of the components of a SWOT Analysis:

Author: Xhienne
This file is licensed under the Creative Commons License. In short: you are free to share and make derivative works of the file under the conditions that you appropriately attribute it, and that you distribute it only under a license identical to this one.

The diagram plainly shows that the most helpful aspects of achieving your goals lie in evaluating your perceived strengths and your perceived opportunities. It also points out the view that strengths are internal which establishes the notion that everything you need is currently within. If that is the case, you must then explore and become familiar with your strengths in order to excel. Take a minute now to stop and list your strongest attributes. Go ahead... I give you permission to write them in the book. After all, you bought it!

MY STRENGTHS/ATTRIBUTES:

_____

_____

_____

_____

_____

Although I have only allotted a few lines for your strengths, you may have many other notable areas in which you do extremely well. Feel free to get another sheet if necessary because the more you think about it, the more strong points you will be able to identify. While this exercise may be easy for some, it may be downright difficult for others as some of us simply don't know which areas are our best. We have been so busy doing and performing tasks without giving thought to our level of skill. For instance, if you were employed as a counselor for 25 years prior to your company's downsizing, then you undoubtedly have a vast amount of knowledge and interpersonal skills that may be useful in alternative areas. So they aren't looking for counselors in your field anymore. Be innovative and match your expertise to areas for which there are opportunities. Good communication skills, extensive human relations skills, proficiency in writing, a gift of compassion, and advanced analytical adeptness all make for a great career in business consulting in any industry. Employ your strengths and avail yourself to new opportunities.

STRENGTHS

Progress toward your goals will be defined as your strengths during this phase. Focus on the positives at this point— even if they seem few. You will be empowered by realizing small victories as you build upon the little things that matter. No matter what you haven't accomplished, there is always one small thing for which you can celebrate and be grateful. For instance, if you are a smoker, and your goal is to quit smoking, you should celebrate the fact that you only had 4 cigarettes today instead of the usual 7 cigarettes/day from last week. That's an improvement, and it shows tremendous strength to abstain from what you normally consume. As you continue to feed and focus on your strengths, they will grow.

Coming back after a six-year hiatus, singer Whitney Houston released a song written by songwriter Diane Warren. The smashing hit, entitled *"I Didn't Know My Own Strength"*, speaks to the challenges we all face and gives us hope to continue even after falling from grace. A portion of the lyrics of the inspirational song declare:

Lost touch with my soul
I had no where to turn
I had no where to go
Lost sight of my dream,
Thought it would be the end of me
I thought I'd never make it through
I had no hope to hold on to,
I thought I would break

I didn't know my own strength
And I crashed down, and I tumbled
But I did not crumble
I got through all the pain
I didn't know my own strength
Survived my darkest hour
My faith kept me alive
I picked myself back up
Hold my head up high
I was not built to break
I didn't know my own strength

Whitney Houston I Didn't Know My Own Strength lyrics found on http://www.directlyrics.com/whitney-houston-i-didnt-know-my-own-strength-lyrics.html

To say that I was inspired upon first hearing this song would be a gross understatement. I can truly say that I was full of many emotions, but what I mostly took away was a cherished assurance of knowing that we were not built to break. Literally speaking, the body has an endless supply of resources to rebuild and recuperate from any insult that might attack us. Everything we need to recover from set-backs, down-falls, and let-downs truly is already inside of us.

Upon deeper discovery and further evaluation, we will find a wealth of hope to pull through and restore that which has been lost. Sometimes rest and recess are the most vital aspects of recovery at a time when the body needs to replenish. Allow me to explain what I am implying here. Because I have a type A personality, most times I operate at 1,000% as I care for the needs of my family, the work of the ministry, the completion of this literary project, the administration of my business, the management of our investment properties, and so on. Whenever I feel as though I am physically drained or depleted due to stress, my body's resistance tends to decrease, and I feel the strain in a number of ways. I usually notice increased fatigue, sinus pressure and obstruction, headaches, and decreased focus. Those who spend a lot of time with me and know me best typically can tell when there is a marked disparity in my performance to which they will make inquiries to find out what's happening with me. They usually spend one whole day asking if I'm alright before I realize that it's time to slow down and rest. I don't require a lot of medication or a trip to the emergency room, but what I tend to do is listen to my body and take the time to stop and let my body replenish. I take action by implementing good measures such as drinking plenty of water, staying in the house, relaxing, and doing the things that I enjoy as much as possible. That's the definition of "*recess.*"

My strength is in organization; therefore I have to take the time to keep *me* together. If my direction is off-center, then I am of no value to those whom I serve. My position is weakened and vulnerable if I continue in a fragmented, unfocused state. Once I decide to take a recess, pretty soon (generally within 1 day off), I am back in the game working at achieving my goals and moving at the speed of lightning to get it all done.

WEAKNESSES

Whenever there is a weakness present in a human, business, or any entity, it is usually a breakdown in the system. Dysfunctions become evident as communication between vital and integral parts lose touch and the delicate balances that are necessary for a smooth, continuous flow detach. I have found the old adage, *"You're only as strong as your weakest link"* to be true. No one enjoys searching out or pin-pointing their weaknesses, but we all have them—even if it's something that is usually considered a positive characteristic. Case in point, if you are so nice and agreeable that you fail to make the hard decisions in favor of the company, this trait may be viewed as a weakness by supervisors. I will not ask you to list your weaknesses here, as I understand how reluctant most individuals may be when it comes to pointing out your "not-so-strong" points. It could take you some time to ponder; however common weaknesses are listed below. See if you can identify with any of them:

- Resistance to change
- Limitations
- Failures
- Helplessness
- Powerlessness
- Vulnerability
- Infirmity
- Frailty
- Indecisiveness

USE YOUR WEAKNESSES

Everyone experiences periods of weakness. As my pastor puts it, "We all live on a fault line, and there is a delicate balance of life as we know it and a disaster just waiting to happen." Remember Mother Theresa whom we mentioned earlier in the section on strength? After her death, it was later revealed in her journals that she privately suffered acute, inner turmoil and uncertainty. Fortunately, she was able to redirect her personal struggles into

74

positive acts to help others. How did she accomplish this? She focused not on herself, but the needs of those around her. Could it be that her personal struggles caused her to sympathize with her neighbors to bring out her innate compassion regarding their plight? If that is the case, then weaknesses are necessary and useful when we are able to recognize them as such, but then use them to meet other objectives.

Weaknesses should be viewed as areas for development and should be minimized by focusing on how we can improve upon them. If you are not strong in a certain area, then you should solicit others to complement you. Seek for those who are strong where you are weak, and attract them to your cause. For example, if you envision publishing a magazine because you are great at writing and organizing copy, but you have no interpersonal skills as to market your product for sale, find a friend whom you can draw upon. The best way to do this is to list your weaknesses and then list the opposite of each alongside of the weakness. You will then know what to look for in others to complement you. Once you know your weaknesses, see if you can think of someone in your life that possesses the attributes which match the opposite of your weaknesses.

Try it now in the table provided below:

CURRENT WEAKNESSES	**OPPOSITE OF WEAKNESSES**
Lack of interpersonal skills	Outgoing, great communication skills
Poor management/organizational skills	Strong administrator, manager, planner
Lack of productivity, originality	Creative, imaginative individual
Procrastinator	Motivated, outgoing, timely character

OPPORTUNITIES AND THREATS

"In the middle of every difficulty lies opportunity."
Albert Einstein

The preceding quote rests among the vast pool of sayings and quotes on opportunity, but simply stated, opportunities are areas that are beneficial or favorable for us to achieve our objectives. In searching out opportunities, we should focus on all the prospects of meeting our goals. If your goal is to achieve gaining profits from the sale of your magazine, ask yourself how can you sell your product in a larger arena? Who is your target market? If it is a magazine that appeals to young people, then you should send advertisements to every school, youth organization, or bookstore. Where do your readers hang out? What events can you attend to promote your product?

If you ask yourself these or similar questions, soon you will see all of the vast opportunities that await you. Sure there will be threats to your success, but see if you can turn the threats into opportunities. Your ability to do so will help you to maximize your opportunities and minimize threats to achieve your goals. In the same manner that we compared the foregoing weakness and the opposite characteristics, we can also balance current opportunities by converting threats.

CHAPTER 8

TIME FOR YOUR PRESCRIPTION

A legendary author, John Harricharan once declared, "Peace is not achieved by controlling nations, but by mastering our thoughts." This single statement profoundly teaches me that everything we desire to achieve, all of the success we experience, and anything which we try to attain, all begin with the thoughts we have.

We allow the enemy to overtake our thoughts, and we forget what we know to be the whole truth. Remember the example of a patient going in for a visit to the physician's office for treatment of a sickness. We go in with a problem, seeking a solution, and we receive what the physician has to say at the time. He gives us information as to what our problem may be, but then he sends us home with a prescription for healing. Now, the prescription is nothing more than a treatment or instructions on how to deal with what is troubling us. If we follow his treatment plan, and if we were to use the prescription that he has ordered, hopefully our problem would soon be resolved; but we can't just follow only a portion of the regimen. We are required to complete the whole course of treatment in order to achieve the desired results. That's the way we need to fight against the enemy.

When he attacks us, why don't we fight back with everything we have been given? When he attacks our mind, why don't we remember the revelations and affirmations we have been given in the past? Why do we give up our peace so easily? When we get

77

overwhelmed, why don't we remember that we are more than conquerors through Him that loved us?

Well I will tell you why. Life comes at us quickly, and the enemy's goal is to overtake us. He tries to overtake our finances, he attempts to overtake our marriages, and certainly he tries to consume our thoughts. If he can show us a picture of us defeated, then he has already won half the battle. If he can steal our focus, and cloud our minds with garbage, then we ultimately feel powerless and stressed just thinking about life's issues. Nothing has even happened yet, but all we can do is think, and think, and think...about the end result of something horrible happening. Our mind works overtime and goes into overload with unnecessary stuff. It's the equivalent of what happens when a computer crashes. There's just too much stuff in the memory, and the computer chips just can't hold everything. When the memory is too full, the device just ultimately gives out. But if we would just delete some of the unnecessary stuff every once in a while—we would have room for the "programs" or information that we want.

Sometime ago, the information technology director of my office told me it was time to update a software program on my computer. During which time, he noticed that I had so many files and unnecessary programs in my computer that I was in danger of losing everything. He then advised me that my computer was likely to crash soon because the memory was "almost full". Now, they tried to explain to me what was going on, but when he started talking about cookies and hanging files, and all sorts of other stuff...I promise you that my mind just shut off because I had the sentiment of "just fix it".

So what they had to do was scan through all the files and programs to see which items could be deleted in order to make room on my memory drive. They told me that it was going to take a while, so I had to sit there and be patient until the computer scanned through to find the corrupt files and delete them. In addition, they explained that I should get rid of any programs that I was not using, such as all of the games and needless downloads that were occupying the useful space on my computer. These measures would have immediate and constructive results as my computer would process faster and more efficient once all of the "junk" was deleted.

Don't you wish life could be more like that? When the memory is "almost full", if we could just go through and hit delete. When our memory is full of things we don't want in our lives, we would just scan through and hit delete. When we have thoughts of anxiety & fear...just scan through and hit delete. Thoughts of people corrupting us...just scan through and hit delete. Thoughts of inadequacy...just scan through and hit delete because you can't afford to have anything in the way of you and your peace. We can't have this stuff cluttering up our systems.

Imagine your creative juices flowing when all of the clutter is removed from the pathways of your peace. When we clutter our hearts with hatred and jealousy and our minds with negative thoughts, it causes us to forget about what we really need. But it's high time we decided to "hit delete" and save our memory space for what's important to us. Don't you realize that you need your memory space for the things that God told you to think about and to create?

RE-PROGRAM YOURSELF

The prolific writer and apostle Paul writes in Philippians 4:8...

Finally, brothers, whatever is true, whatever is noble, whatever is right, whatever is pure, whatever is lovely, whatever is admirable— if anything is excellent or praiseworthy—think about such things.

With everything in your being, you must re-program yourself to master your thoughts to control every situation in your life. Our thoughts are the only antidotes we have against the poisonous notions of the enemy. That is how we counteract what he's trying to shove down our throats, so that should be our prescription for peace. The plan has already been provided for us, but I encourage you to be diligent in your thinking and mastering your thoughts.

God gives us hope and compels us to believe Him for the next situation or the overwhelming things that we are facing right now. You know the things that seem like they are so significant that they are about to overtake us and cause us to give in? But right before you have the opportunity to get scared and allow fear to cripple you— why don't you stop and think for a minute. We need to stop and remember the past victories and believe that God will take us through the battle at hand.

When the enemy declared war on the children of Israel, it was King Jehoshaphat who called the people together to fast and pray and to seek the face of the LORD on what they should do. He, as their leader, began to pray, and in his prayer, he began to remember and remind the Lord of the marvelous acts He had done for Israel in the past. He began to tell the Lord who He was to him acknowledging that only God could save them in their current situation. Now, you've got to think that God had not forgotten who He was. Why is Jehosephat reminding Him? Because after all, not only is God all-powerful, but He is all-knowing. He is sovereign!

But here was Jehoshaphat, a skillful leader, standing before the people seemingly reminding God, but what he was really doing was reminding the people of what God had already done. The children of Israel believed, but Jehoshaphat, their king and prophet had to let them hear it in order to have them think on it. He wanted to increase their faith as the Word of God says…"faith comes by hearing."

We can get to a place of victory if we use the right prescription. We are all trying to get to a place of peace in our lives. Well since some of us don't feel better until we take a few pills, I have a few for you. You want to live a life of peace with nothing missing, nothing lacking, and nothing broken? You want to know how to achieve 100% while you are going through your test? Well, here is the prescription laid forth in Philippians 4.

1. Pray Your Way Through
Firstly, you must *pray* your way through. Paul said…Be anxious for nothing, but in everything by prayer and supplication. Pray for direction and peace regarding any situation.

2. Petition for What you Need
Similar to prayer, a petition is rooted in asking, however it goes further. When you make a petition, you earnestly and

fervently make your appeal as in pleading your cause. You want to know where to get strength in the midst of your storm? You have got to *petition* the one who made you and who knows all about you. He is waiting on you to ask Him for what you need. He's here to help you, and you should turn to Him for everything you need?

3. Praise Your Way Through
You've got to *praise* your way through. That's the "thanksgiving" part. You've got to praise Him and recognize that the end of your problem is at the starting point of your praise or gratefulness to Him.

4. Ponder Your Way to Peace
This is just another way of saying we have to remember and think on these things. That's what keeps us in perfect peace in times of recession and reorganization. God said, "And I will keep him in perfect peace whose mind is stayed on thee."

So let's review this. According to Paul, you've got to pray, you've got to petition, you must give thanksgiving or praise, and finally, you must ponder. When the enemy tries to steal our faith by catching us off-guard, **we can't forget to remember!** We can't forget to remind ourselves of what God has done for us in the past. Believe and have faith that if he did it back then— He **will** do it again.

Healing takes time, and patience is required, but if you are willing to wait on God in earnest expectation, He will reward you. If you have ever earnestly asked God to do something really great, you know what it means to persevere and endure. He has freely given us the promise, but the patience to hold out comes with a price. As you build your tolerance, you come to appreciate the purpose and plan for the wait. God's desire is that we would grow and get everything out of each experience. Sometimes, it's not about the destination, but it's all about what you will learn and experience along the journey. I used to say, "Don't worry about the road traveled...just focus on where you are going." However, my perspective has changed. If I didn't pay attention to the journey, imagine how much I would have missed. I would have no content for this book. I am now thankful for the good and the bad experiences, because it has made me who I am. It took a while to get here, but the "new and improved me" is more equipped to handle this level.

PATIENCE AND PREPARATION

When I think of all the hasty and impulsive decisions I have made in the past along the journey to my dreams, I usually cringe with repugnance. I have definitely made bad decisions as it relates to prior investments, relationships, and even career choices, but I am thankful that I was able to recover and move on. All things being considered, I have come to realize that it was a lack of patience and preparation at the core of all the bad decisions. Had I carefully planned and thought about the alternatives, I would have made better choices along the way. I know that I am not alone in this sentiment, as I watch many people today make the same hasty decisions. On some occasions, I am able to help them to better prepare and avoid the same experiences I encountered, but there are individuals who must experience the tough lessons before they are willing to listen to reason. In those instances, I say as my mother always says: "Bought sense is the best sense."

If you are not willing to take the time to research and prepare for what you desire, you will soon find yourself paying for lessons you never wanted to learn. But if you are focused on preparing and organizing your goals, you will become patient enough to wait and pass on the ideas and plans of others who wish to involve you to get what they want. I have often received proposals and offers to participate in business ventures with people who want to make fast money. They usually want my time, talents, or treasure to facilitate their dreams, and I am not opposed to helping them, but I now understand my limitations. My husband's philosophy has helped to keep me focused. He once told me to review my intentions each time I am confronted with a proposal to see if it is in alignment with my personal goals. If the idea or plan does not fit or it fails to propel me toward my desires, then I pass. I have developed the patience to wait on what is right for me. Forcing deals and stressing over what does not work is a thing of the past. Most times, we become too involved in the dreams and aspirations of others which may cause us to get off track when it comes to accomplishing what we want. To this end, I would caution you to also realize your limitations, and never be afraid to say when you have reached your point of assistance. Remember, if you are too overwhelmed and bogged down with the concerns of others, how will you achieve what you want to achieve for you?

CHAPTER 9

IT'S ABOUT TIME

*"So God blessed Noah and his sons, and said unto them, be
fruitful, and multiply, and fill the earth."*
Genesis 9:1 — New King James Version

Ever wonder when it is going to finally be *'your time?'* After all you've gone through and the seeds you have sown, doesn't it seem that sometimes God is taking too long to get to you? Sometimes it seems as though He has boxed you in and shut you up in an uncomfortable and isolated place to deal with a mess you didn't even create.

This passage of scripture, taken from the bible, is a direct commandment given to one of the most famous characters within the Word of God after he had gone through a tough season. Noah, the only one found righteous in a world gone astray, would be the one chosen to replenish the earth after its destruction by flood. Because of his unrelenting obedience to God, he and his entire family were saved in the midst of God's plan to wipe out the whole human race for their evil ways.

You know how the story goes if you have taken the time to pick up the bible and read just a few pages, for his story is deemed the most talked about account of God's power and supremacy since the creation of man. Even if you have not read Noah's story in the bible, you have undoubtedly seen pictures of the ark. There are nursery

84

scenes and coloring books depicting the setting of a wonderful backdrop with a well-constructed boat made by Noah's hands and a beautiful world with green grass, the shinning sun, and animals willingly going into the ark two by two. Everything seems wonderful. Talk about the calm before the storm, but the truth of the matter is this: The earth would be destroyed in just a few days, and it was a horrible thing. God, in His omnipotence had created man in His image, given him power over the earth, and watched him fall from grace.

What would make God repent in His decision of ever creating man? Imagine the frustration within God's patience as He waited on man to obey Him, yet man's disobedience continued to abound until God's mercy would no longer accommodate it. The result? God would destroy all that displeased Him and save those whom He would later use to give Him glory. Because after all, that's what this whole thing is about. God seeks out those whom will give Him glory.

WILL GOD RECEIVE THE GLORY?

This may be an alarming statement for you, but God is not concerned about your intellect. Neither is He impressed with all that you have personally achieved if He doesn't get the glory. He wants you to use all of your resources and everything you have within to bless Him. It's all about the glory of the one who created us all. All that you have accomplished, and anything that you have acquired was only by the mercy of God, and He is only motivated by what gives Him glory. He only gets in what gives Him glory. So if you are planning to do anything, and you are unsure about it... ask yourself one simple question. Will God receive any glory? If you want to reap anything for your labor and get any kind of long-term return on your investment, you first better ask yourself if God can find any glory in it.

So Noah found favor with the LORD, and he and his family were chosen to be saved. Because Noah was the only one walking in obedience, he was chosen to remain alive in the midst of a terrible storm. But before he could be saved, there was just one more act of obedience which the LORD required of him. God told Noah to build an ark in which He would later enclose them in order to protect and provide for them as He executed His plan to destroy what no longer served Him. God knew that He could no longer get the glory out of His creation, so saddened by this reality; He assessed and diagnosed the situation, devised a plan, and intervened upon the earth. You will take notice that even God takes the time to plan whenever He sets out to accomplish anything. He who is sovereign and rules the entire universe conceives of a plan and carries it out through those who will trust and obey him.

TRUST VS. OBEY

Trusting and obeying God are the two prerequisites to reaping in times of recession. Although God had caused everything else in the world to fall and collapse around Noah, He kept Noah safe, and that is what He will do for you in uncertain times—in times of economic collapse—if you will trust and obey Him. Now why is it that I say trust and obey? These terms, although utilized interchangeably vary in their definition and should not be used synonymously because they are two totally different concepts. We trust in a multiplicity of people, things, and beliefs even if we do not obey them. For instance, you may trust that your car will get you from point A to point B every time you start the engine, but if you do not obey the maintenance schedule or those maintenance lights alerting you to do what it takes to care for your vehicle; your car will not bring you about much further. The two work hand in hand, and in order for you to reap what you want, you must do both.

To trust is to believe or hope with a strong conviction in that which you depend upon to be true and accurate. It takes confidence and expectation to trust in anything, but how is it developed? I submit that trust is learned and developed through our experiences. Specifically, we are taught, for the most part, what we should believe regarding our faith or alliances. We learn, over time, what is reliable and what is true. The only way we could ever come to trust a God that we could not see, is to have an experience with Him or be taught about Him. We trust Him because of what we have experienced in our past and through the witnesses of others.

"This is the confidence we have in approaching God: that if we ask anything according to his will, he hears us. And if we know that he hears us—whatever we ask—we know that we have what we asked of him."

I John 5:14-15— New International Version

When we ask God for our desires, we are confident that He will grant our requests because we perceive that He has answered in the past. So if we ask again, we trust that He will again respond to that which we ask of Him. Alternatively, when we obey, He trusts that we will do exactly as He asks of us. He wants to see if you will follow His commands in order that He might accomplish His plans within the earth realm. To obey is to follow instructions or behave in accordance with a law, rule, or order (*Encarta Dictionary, English North America*).

We want what God has, but we refuse to follow the laws he has in place for us to prosper. In order for Noah to be saved, he had to trust and obey God. He could have trusted that God would save him from the flood just by staying in his home. Why did he need to build an ark to be saved? What if He would have questioned God and not followed every step of the instructions that were given? Would he have died in the flood also? It was a simple act of obedience that led Noah to go ahead and build the ark without a single sign of rain. The people of Noah's day thought that the earth had been cursed because it hadn't rained for years, and they were made to toil with the ground to harvest any crops. But Noah obeyed despite the climate around him. He obeyed in the face of criticism and doubt from the people around him. Noah trusted and obeyed God, but can you imagine how hard it must have been for him to do that?

Just think of Noah's time on the ark. The bible records that he and his family were on the ark a little over a year. I know you thought it was 40 days and 40 nights, but that's just how long the rain fell. The earth was covered with water long after that, and there was no way they could exit the boat until they were certain that it was dry.

So understand this, they are on the boat for a year, and you must know that this was no Carnival Cruise. They are on the ship with pairs of every kind of breathing animal— domestic and wild, large and small— along with birds and flying insects of every kind. Does this sound like a trip to the zoo to you? Well, it sounds as if God set up Noah and his family to deal with a mess. Sure Noah started out doing fine, and walking in obedience, but I just believe that there were uncertain days—maybe just a few—but there had to be days when Noah thought to himself... what in the world is going on? This is what I have to endure for trying to live righteously? Why do I have to deal with all of this, and when will it all cease?

MAKING IT THROUGH A MESS

When you find yourself in the midst of a mess you didn't create; it makes it even harder to deal with the situation. From whence do you gain the strength to go through? Noah had to be a strong person to deal with all that was happening on that boat. Think about the conflicts of people on top of people, animals without the ability to reason, and the fear of the unknown. He had to struggle with uncertainty regarding where they were headed. What a mess! What else can you do? You trust and obey God with your uncertainties for now is the time to reap, but you will never reap if you can't see yourself making it through. Pray for the grace and favor you need to continue. Remind God of the promises He made to keep you safe when everything else around you is dying. He can keep you in the midst of it all. Even in the midst of the mess, He is able to keep you until the overwhelming waters are over. You may feel closed in and boxed in now, but you are safe in His arms. You can rest assured that He didn't shut you up if He didn't plan to bring you out.

Now is the time to regroup and encourage yourself. Faith comes by hearing, so when you are faced with adversity; you have to talk yourself through. Words are never intimidated by the obstacles that we face. Even if we don't fully believe all that we are saying, our words render hope for us to take the next step to keep going until we are able to get out. There are 3 vital steps that Noah performed in order to get to a time of reaping, and I believe they are essential for us carry out if we are to ever experience life the way God intended.

SACRIFICE

Upon being released from the ark, the first act Noah performed was to sacrifice. He built an altar and sacrificed the animals and birds which had been approved for that purpose. The bible declares that the LORD was pleased with the sacrifice, so much so, that he made a covenant regarding the entire earth.

That's the first step for us. If you are asserting that now is the time for you to finally prosper, it should start with sacrifice. You will not receive different results if you consistently perform in the same manner. What is it that's holding you back from moving ahead? Whether it is a commitment to sacrifice time, money, or other resources, you must forgo that which has stolen your focus in the past and caused you to forfeit your harvest.

BE FRUITFUL AND MULTIPLY

Secondly, the next command given to Noah by God was to be fruitful and multiply. To be fruitful implies productivity. No other concept brings about abundance and profitability than to work toward being fruitful. God supplied all of what Noah and his family needed when they got off of the ark, but His intention was for them to take that which He supplied and cause it to multiply. As I write this passage, I am reminded of the horrific times that we, the citizens of New Orleans, experienced in the aftermath of Hurricanes Katrina and Rita.

During August of 2005, the two most devastating storms ripped through Southeast Louisiana, the Mississippi Gulf Coast, and regions of Alabama leaving billions of dollars in damages, lost lives, and flooded properties. Many had evacuated and were carried safely to neighboring cities and adjacent states, but it was a nightmare to live through it. Families were torn apart, small children were snatched out of their familiar surroundings, and life as we knew it, ceased to be the same. Since my personal home was spared total destruction by flooding, my husband decided to give officers who had lost everything a place to live until they could figure out how to rebuild. He describes it as a bitter-sweet experience as he was thankful that we hadn't lost it all, but he couldn't help but feel sympathetic to his fellow officers. While he wanted to bring my children and I back home right away, he requested that we stay where we were for the time being as he really didn't want to rush the guys out of the house. What could I say? God had brought us safely through it all. We were forced to trust and obey God as never before, and when the storms were over, we still could not return to life as usual. It took a long time for the waters to recede and the infrastructure of the city to be rebuilt. Therefore, I understood that we had to remain where we were until it was safe to move forward in the next phases of our lives. Sounds familiar?

For the period following the storms, there were limited jobs and resources. Because we were displaced, we were in a new land and dependent upon God and anyone whom He sent to help us. Initially, it seemed like a bad place to be, but pretty soon, I started to see the blessing in it all. I was off from work (indefinitely), I received resources such as food, gift cards, and care packages from people whom I had never met, and I was around family and friends who tried everything to ensure that we stayed in good spirits. Each night, they would have dinners for all of us to eat and fellowship together. It was like a family reunion every single day. After the first month, I decided to do something I had always wanted to do but never had the time because of my demanding career. I enrolled in a real estate course and obtained my license within just 3 months.

God had revealed to me something very simple but profound. Once the waters receded, there would be people moving back to New Orleans, and they would need somewhere to live. Even if they had decided not to return, former residents would need to sell their homes. Well, wouldn't you know it... that's exactly what happened? The real estate business really boomed for a season, and even when the rest of the country was experiencing a serious downturn, New Orleans was insulated from the initial shocks of the slump because there were so many investors and grants given to rebuild the storm-ravaged parishes. I was blessed to buy and sell many properties, and I was able to help my friends and family return home. They returned when deals were great, and they purchased properties that they may have been unable to afford prior to the storms and the influx of insurance claims received. God blessed them with money and a new outlook on life.

During this time, I met so many people who were uncertain about what they were to do. I also met investors who wanted quick sales, so they offered me properties with no money down to ensure their efforts to swiftly cut all ties within New Orleans. It was a win/win situation, and it was about time to rebuild and reap. I was determined to rebuild my life and assist as many people as possible in their quest to do the same.

Although it was viewed as the worst time in history for many New Orleanians, there are a few of us with a different story. It was a time for me to reap because I trusted and obeyed the voice of God. He commanded me to be fruitful and multiply, and He blessed my efforts by rewarding me with commissions and several properties for pennies on the dollar. He has caused me to prosper, and if I am to be truly honest with myself, the first few years following the storms were filled with abundance. Most of the citizens prospered tremendously as we received more money in larger proportions than ever before. There were also scores of buyers approved for business and auto loans during this time of rebuilding.

REPLENISH

While I think the economic events and housing boom that ensued in the aftermath of Katrina was God's way of blessing us, I don't think He ever intended for us to be excessive in our spending and financing. Somehow we got caught up into buying things just because we could. But then, the housing market crash came our way, and we were not ready for it. We were experiencing a surplus and multiplied resources, but I'm not sure how many were being good stewards over the resources we were given.

Whenever we are supplied with abundance, we must remember to be good stewards and avoid lavish spending or ludicrous stockpiling. We can still win without being wasteful, but we must not hoard what should be invested to replenish our resources for future use. The last command given to Noah and his family was to replenish the earth. God not only wanted them to sacrifice their time and resources and be fruitful and multiply; but He wanted them to replenish the earth.

Keep in mind, all of the earth's resources had been depleted in the flood, and it was up to Noah and his family to save a little of what was supplied in order to re-plant for a later harvest. How does all this apply to our present-day situation? Allow me to explain using a simple economical technique called "just-in-time" (JIT) inventory management.

Created by one of the biggest and greatest American corporations, Wal-mart's just-in-time (JIT) inventory method allows them to have just enough supply at any given moment to meet their customers' demands. In short, they do not want to have shelves full of inventory without immediate buyers; however they do not desire to have buyers coming in looking for products that they don't have. That would not be profitable. Likewise, we cannot hold onto and store all of our resources never sowing anything, but then we cannot spend everything depleting our reserves as well. What's the solution? We have to plant and manage realizing that God is our source. After all, that's the only way to reap. Suze Orman has a great way of describing this concept as she says, "I believe that each one of us is, in effect, a glass, in that we can hold only so much; after that, the water—or the money—just goes down the drain."

If you have been faithful in managing and being productive over the resources that you already have, then it is your time to be rewarded. You cannot continue to give and be a good steward without God noticing your efforts. Now is the time for you to reap.

CHAPTER 10

A TIME TO REAP

"And my God shall supply all your need
according to His riches in glory by Christ Jesus."
Philippians 4:19— New King James Version

On a routine visit to the grocery store one day, I received an awesome revelation as I observed my children in the checkout line. Oh, you know how it goes. All of that candy at the checkout counter is a set up, and something must be done about it. As I was checking out, my six year old daughter asked for something, and my reply to her was…"Get what you want." Immediately her countenance lifted as she began to put several items on the counter. To my surprise, my 10 year old son started to scold her as he said, "Tayler, you can't have all of that." He continued, "I'm not expecting Momma to buy all of this candy for me, but I have my own money, and I'm going to buy what I want for myself."

But then my youngest said something that caught my attention. She responded to him…"Did you not hear Momma say, "Get what you want?"

Now here is what she understood that he did not. I had the money to grant her request. She only had 50 cents with her, but that which she had; she placed it in my hands. Although it wasn't nearly enough to cover what she had placed on the counter, she placed what she had in my hands. It didn't matter that her allowance wasn't suf-

93

ficient to supply all of her desires. She understood her connection to me, and she knew that it was doable.

That's what many of us need to do. Stop looking at an allowance because it's not enough anyway. We are so worried about the allowance, but God says...."I operate in abundance." Instead of looking at what we have and operating alone trying to rationalize and make the small amount work, we've got to realize that when we give it to God, and ask Him according to his will, we can have what we want. So we give our seed to him, and he causes us to walk in favor.

Sticking with the source implies walking in the character of God and allowing Him to use you as a resource to accomplish His purposes in the earth realm. Yes, He will supply all of our need, but His desire is that we would supply the needs of those around us and somehow win them over for the cause of Christ. Can He use you as a vessel to bless someone else? Could it be that He will not release His abundance unto us until He can trust us to share and be a resource to others?

Just recently during our family movie time, I had the pleasure of seeing a wonderful story about an affluent family taking in and caring for a homeless boy. Although a total stranger to them, the wife's tenacious actions and blind love for humanity ignited change for the better in many lives and within their community. The award-winning movie, entitled *The Blindside*, was a great enactment of unconditional love and the power of giving in the true life story of Michael Oher who currently plays football for a professional NFL franchise. Because someone else was willing to sow what God had granted unto them, they became a resource. That's one of the essential keys to abundance, and that is how we can stay connected to the source. Imagine being that kind of giver. Imagine walking in that type of power and financial freedom, but possessing the freedom to share it all.

When you find security and trust in God knowing that He is the source of everything we could possibly want, it is amazing what we are willing to share. It is amazing what we would give if we understood that the source is an endless, infinite reservoir of that which we need to survive and prosper. I may not be what some may consider rich at this point in my life, but I certainly know that I am connected to the one who is.

If we can only come to realize that God is our source, and money is only a resource, we would fight with everything in our being to stay connected to the source. He is the foundation for all that we may build or any wealth that we can amass; therefore the unstable economy should not determine our stability. You cannot hope to recover, rebuild, or reap unless your hope is tapped into the source of every good and perfect gift. Whenever my resources seem to be near depletion, I return to the source of it all, and soon enough all of my needs are met, my finances are flowing; and no matter what changes take place within the economy, I reap a harvest.

Just recently, I had a conversation with a good friend, and she was simply telling me how grateful she was. Her face was exuding with peace as she stated, "I don't worry about my bills anymore, I just trust God, and I'm grateful." That's also a very powerful key to reaping—you have to be grateful, and you've got to say how grateful you are. "Grateful for what?" you may say.

GRATEFULNESS IS THE KEY

If you have been through a lot, and you feel that you have experienced great loss, find a way to be grateful for what you have left. Be grateful for another day. Be grateful for the next opportunity. Be grateful for this time in your life because although you may be experiencing lack, there is no lack or shortage in God. He can supply you with enough to start all over again, and for that, you should be grateful. "Gratitude decreases stress hormones" and has been attributed to noted boosts in physical health and overall well-being according to Dr. Michael Roizen, Chief Wellness Officer and co-author of *YOU: The Owner's Manual.*

In regards to negative outcomes and adverse health conditions, many wellness experts will encourage you to *"think"* yourself healthy as there is definitely a direct connection in the way you think and your physical condition. However I say, you can also *"thank"* yourself healthy as there is a direct connection in your level of gratitude and your overall condition. As I stated earlier on, we are all intricately woven together like a well-oiled system connected to one another. Like the systems and organs of the body, we are all dependant on each other to properly function. This idea had particular resonance for me as I learned about the crisis in Greece and its relationship to our U.S. economy.

As Wall Street started to appreciate an upswing from the crash of 2007-2008, in our economic standing, Greece started experiencing financial woes in 2009-2010; but it had direct implications for us. Within a few weeks, the DOW index had dropped several hundred points, and investors were worried again about our economic status. But what did their struggles have to do with us?

According to a related article on finance and economics, "Stock markets around the world have slumped as investors fret about the financial stability of a region that makes up almost a quarter of the world economy" *(The Economist, May 8ᵗʰ, 2010).* Here again, this is a testament to the fact that we cannot depend solely on the world economy or other external factors as safety nets for our success. Major areas of the economy have started to show signs of recovery, but every aspect must experience improvement because the entire system makes up the whole. Let's remember that the creator of it all is still in control.

Although we are connected to each other, it is important that we remember the source. When one system seems to be malfunctioning, it is imperative that the others compensate and return to the source of it all. Since God is the center of all that we hope for or desire, He should be considered as our source. After all, He supplies all of our needs if only we would acknowledge him as the source and ask for his guidance. Unlike countries and governments attempting to dig their way out of recessions, He already has a plan. He doesn't need stimulus packages or austerity programs that may or may not prove beneficial. He already has a specific system, and now is the time to use it. Now is the time to get connected to the source, work your plan, and reap what you always desired.

Refuse to dwell on your past mistakes and the past losses. Now is the time to forge forward and focus on the finish. Expect what will happen next, and look forward to what is expecting you. Now is the time to be open to new ideas and opportunities, and look for those who have the ability to help you bring your dreams to reality! Think of the countless medical survivors who have overcome terminal illnesses although external environmental conditions were unfavorable. The reason is....healing comes from within. So stop feeling sorry for yourself and blaming everything on the economy. You were living just fine when you had no idea of the ripping downturn.

SO WHAT'S THE NEXT STEP?

Ask yourself..."What is the next step or phase for me?" Just the thought of getting out of your regular routine should amuse you. You may want to ask a friend or mentor what they have done to bounce back or overcome their challenging periods.

Sometimes, just hearing a story of triumph and perseverance is enough to ignite the fuel or stir up something within you. I am often motivated to great lengths when I listen to some successful person's life story or the biographical documentaries telling how some world icon grew up poor and discounted by their peers only to later emerge as a prolific leader within their industry. I then ask myself, "What's stopping me?" What's the difference between me and the next successful person?" During those times, I soon come to realize that it has little to do with education or any other skill or learned behavior. On the contrary, it has everything to do with passion. Therefore, the question then evolves... "Am I going after my dream and goals with enough passion and perseverance— enough to really see them through?

That is a valid question, and it is a question that you must consider before you can ask for anything from anyone else. If you are not willing to give your all and pursue your dreams with passion, you are asking for mediocrity every time. I implore you to push pass the urge to be average, because average people don't reap supernatural abundance. Maybe their needs are met, but these uncertain times call for more than mediocrity. Think about it. If your corporation is forced to downsize, like so many American companies have recently done, I guarantee you the decisions on who will be retained and who will be released all come down to those who have the most passion. Corporate decision-makers will ask the hard questions like, "Which individuals consistently perform with excellence?" Who is able to cross-train and perform multiple tasks?"

As an administrator, I am gravely annoyed by mediocrity or half-hearted service. My kids will also readily attest to the fact that I constantly drill them on performing every assigned task with fervor and confidence. Again, ask yourself why you are doing what you are doing because if it is not worth your intense pursuit, you should not do it at all. I also point out to my kids that people can sense when you are not whole-heartedly into what you are doing. If they do not sense your enthusiasm, then they are less likely to be into you. Your face should exude joy, and your conversation should be one of positive affirmation when you speak of your goals or particular interests. When you give everything you've got, and when you speak positively about your dreams, you are in a unique position to ask. But remember to ask with confidence.

Now this is the confidence that we have in Him, that if we ask anything according to His will, He hears us. And if we know that He hears us, whatever we ask, we know that we have the petitions that we have asked of Him.

I John 5:14-15

Of all the words contained within the preceding scripture, I believe the most important and significant of them all is the word "ask". Although unassuming and seemingly insignificant, its three-letter context entails great capacity, for there is enormous power in merely asking. Just a simple request can change multitudes as it saves time, money, and even lives. Allow me to explain why I feel this way.

Throughout the course of my work week, there are several times within the implementation of my duties in which I ask. Whether it's delegating a task to my assistants or asking a seller for concessions on a contract, I frequently must make requests in order to effectively perform or accomplish my responsibilities. I ask my kids to pick up after themselves. I ask my mother to help with the kids, and I ask my husband for backrubs... all with the confidence in knowing that if I ask, I will most likely receive that which I have requested. Because I have a relationship and an understanding with those whom I may ask,

I am never fearful or reluctant to ask. How else would I get all these things I desire? Therefore, I am never afraid or reluctant to ask my creator for anything. I am certain that He is willing and able to perform any task, give any good gift, and grant any request that I may have. All too often, many people fail to obtain what they desire or get where they want to be simply because they refuse to ask for what they want, or most unfortunately, they don't ask or operate with confidence.

I have witnessed this type of confidence personified with a friend of mine who usually has enough confidence to walk into a room and seem as though he is in charge—no matter where he goes. It's not the kind of confidence that comes across as arrogance or haughtiness, but he walks in knowing what he wants and where he is trying to be; and it always works out for him. For instance, if we are attending a large conference, he can walk in late to find the auditorium full of thousands of delegates who all had the noble intention of arriving early to secure good seats close to the platform. Somehow he always strolls casually to the front, as though he is part of the planning committee, and he procures the seats that everyone else was afraid to take. It works every single time because no one would dare to ask him if he is a delegate or part of the hosting team.

DON'T BE AFRAID TO ASK

My estimation is many people fail to obtain what they desire simply because they are afraid to ask for what they want. Maybe it's because they have experienced rejection or some type of negative result in the past, or they were incorrectly taught...If you want something, do it yourself. Well, I could not disagree more. As I mentioned earlier, relationships and resources are everything, and you can not allow your past experiences and beliefs to stop you from asking. But this is not the time to ask insignificant, meaningless questions. I mean, ask the hard things. Make powerful, absurd requests if you really want to see change and make a positive impact in your life. Don't worry about the responses to your requests at this point, for your lack of confidence will be conveyed as weakness; and no one is attracted to that. Have confidence and assertiveness in your asking, and wait on a "yes".

One time, I wrote a purchase agreement contract for one of my real estate clients. Within the contract, we decided to ask the seller to pay 6% or the equivalent of $12,000.00 in closing costs for the purchaser. This would significantly reduce the amount of cash the purchaser would need during the closing of the transaction if the seller agreed. My client, the purchaser was somewhat apprehensive when I suggested that we ask for such a great amount because she really wanted the home, and she did not want to seem as though she was "low-balling" or playing games with the seller. I advised her that it was ultimately her decision as the client, and I was legally bound to write whatever she requested. I also pointed out that all we could do is ask to get a feel for how the seller would respond.

Upon presenting the contract to the seller's agent, she seemed apprehensive to the large amount, and implied that her client may be reluctant to agree to it. My reply to her was… "All we can do is ask." I advised her to present the offer as written and get back to me with her client's decision. Being confident that we were in a "buyer's market" and knowing the climate of the market, I was convinced that we would receive what we were requesting. I was looking at the big picture although my client only had a view from their specific transaction. This seller's property had been on the market for 308 days, and I knew they were motivated. I also knew that other homes in the same block had been on the market for quite some time with no activity or interest from buyers. I also knew that the list price per square foot was well above the average price per square foot than those homes which had recently sold.

Well wouldn't you know it? The seller granted full approval and paid the $12,000.00 towards the purchaser's closing costs. Now you understand why you need a good realtor? Even when you are afraid to ask, you should align yourself with someone who will. Think of all the money and rewards you could have reaped if you had only asked. I know I could have saved a lot more when I bought my first property had I known to ask for a few more concessions from the seller. Clearly, this proves that what you don't know can hurt you and cost you. It can cost you time, heartache, and money.

Another reason we are unwilling to ask for what we want is pride. Because we want to give the illusion that all is well with us, we are averse to ask for anything. A separate client of my real estate business wanted to prove to me and the seller how much money she had. She refused to ask for closing costs or any discounts because she didn't need it. She was accustomed to "paying for what she wanted". She wanted the best, and she had the money to pay for it. Maybe I will understand that phenomenon later in life, but for now...$12,000.00 remaining in my account looks better to me than writing a big check to prove a point.

All too often, we confuse pride with confidence, and we fail the tests of life. Scott Wilson, author of *The Next Level* says: "Lessons on pride and humility aren't easy ones. They often require radical spiritual surgery and long periods of rehabilitation." If you somehow feel stagnated and stuck in a holding pattern where you are unable to recover, could it be that you are failing this test? We should not confuse confidence with pride and arrogance because you may be repelling what you desire and prolonging your journey to your dream.

No one is attracted to arrogance. It only compels people to wish on bringing you down a peg or two. Arrogance is haughtiness which is the opposite of humility. Even God resists the proud and calls it an abomination to Him. Arrogance is conceit and an attitude of condescension which capitalizes on the weaknesses and flaws of others. It should never be confused with confidence. By contrast, confidence is self-assurance and self-reliance in the belief that you are sufficient. All of your skills and training have made you who you are, and that makes you worth knowing. There is no need to cause others to feel bad or seem insufficient when you know who you are.

CAPTITALIZE ON CONVERSATIONS

Aside from asking a lot of requests everyday, I also noticed how many questions people tend to ask me on a daily basis. One day, I decided to journal the amount and content of the questions I received and noted that the questions ranged from inquiries about my family to more specific questions about my wardrobe preferences. Have you ever noticed that questions are real conversation-starters? For instance, I can wear a really hot pair of shoes, and I guarantee you that 75% of the women, and sometimes even men, will comment or ask something about the shoes. Once they ask the question, the conversation usually evolves into how cute they are, the comfort level of the shoes, the price of the shoes, and then finally, where did I purchase the shoes. I can take the conversation anywhere from this point, and on many occasions, I have. Can you see how I could take a conversation on my shoe purchase and preference into a discussion on a home purchase? If you can, then you can do it just as easily. My husband would say that I am just finding any excuse to explain my shoe fetish, but I say it's all connected. I agree with Cinderella... One shoe really can change a person's life!

But on a more serious note, you can do it too, and it is the easiest thing to do if you would just think about it. I also wear my real estate name tag to all grocery stores, hospitals, and especially to my children's schools. You may not be surprised at the amount of questions I get regarding real estate business every time I wear it. It's a small item, but it attracts people to me, and once they ask a question... I have a conversation with them in which I start to ask questions. They never know that I am selling the whole time because I don't start out talking about showing them houses. I start out asking questions about what interests they have. If you have ever done this, you recognize that people love to talk about what they are doing and what interests them. They can go on and on for hours, and if you will take the time to listen; you can achieve your goals and sell what you offer as you capitalize on the conversation.

I understand that time is money, and now that there isn't a lot of money at your disposal, now is the time to spend what you do have, and that is time. Believe me, I hear what some may say..."I don't have a lot of time either." Well, you better find the time to participate in conversations. How will you build your business or even pursue your passion if you don't take the time to do it. Nothing will happen over night, and we would be inaccurate to think that successful businesses and self-made millionaires did it that way. On the contrary, I am certain most of them will testify that the ultimate key to their success is the amount of time and commitment they invested in whatever their passion happens to be.

If you are not willing to spend time asking questions like, "What can I do to promote my business?", and "where can I find my target audience?" you will soon be compelled to ask questions with the following content: "Who can I call to help me pay my light bill?" or "When am I ever going to get another commission check?" I don't like asking questions like that, and neither should you. Let me say it again. If you want to recover and reap, you have to be willing to ask the pertinent questions that propel you into action and prompt you to thinking... "What can I do now to improve my situation?"

I once heard a speaker describe the fascinating concept on the power of asking yourself a question. He explained, "When you verbally pose a question to your brain, subconsciously the brain immediately begins to seek out answers; and it does not stop until it finds the answer." How amazing is that? Now you understand how powerful it is to simply ask. It is a part of the process, and it is absolutely necessary to do it.

ASK ...AND YOU SHALL RECEIVE

It's not just a catchy saying, but it is a commandment from the bible of which you may or may not be familiar. Because it is biblically sound, I have done it simply to test God's word, and it works for me over and over again. Not only do I ask myself the hard questions about what I want, but I also find myself asking others about things that perplex me. I always ask with the expectation that I will receive an answer. I ask hoping that I will receive a positive response, and for the most part, I am happily rewarded. Yes, there are times when the answers or outcomes are not favorable, but if I keep the right perspective, I will gain something from my asking— even if it is no more than the knowledge of dealing with various kinds of personalities or people in general. I win, and I reap something no matter what! If you will determine to view life this way, I promise that you will begin to receive more of what you want.

CHAPTER 11

A TIME TO ASK

I am inquisitive by nature, so I have never had a problem asking questions. That may be the reason it was so easy for me to grasp the concept of "Ask and ye shall receive." When I was in grade school, my mother had the occasion to visit all of my 5th grade teachers during parent-teacher conference time. To date, she still remembers the dominant concern which most of my teachers discussed related to my participation in class. They all had the same complaint about me. "She asks too many questions". That's all they had to say? That's your complaint?!

Well, no one could tell that my excessive curiosity would prove beneficial as they were apparently annoyed by my inquisitive nature...maybe because they did not know the answers. But I have come to know that who you ask is just as important as what you ask. Why waste time asking someone who does not know the answers? God always knows the answer, and He is able to give you divine directions to your destiny. What do I mean by that? Allow me to expound a little further... God has already been there. Because He is Alpha and Omega, He has predestined us for His purpose; therefore He knows the place, He knows the plan, and if we should ask Him, He would open up to us good treasure.

When I think of the gifts and treasures He has placed within us, I am reminded of one of the most famous productions of all times, *The Wizard of Oz.*

Now don't turn me off. Stay tuned for what I am getting ready to say next. If you know the story of *The Wizard of Oz,* you will remember the main characters, Dorothy, the Tin Man, the Lion, and the Scarecrow. Each of them had their own perceived insufficiencies which led them on a search for answers. Their lone and uncertain journey down the yellow brick road would inevitably lead them to the Wizard who would in turn make them all better. Come on, you remember the story. The Lion was in search of courage, the Tin Man needed a heart, and the scarecrow had a desperate desire for a brain. For some time, they traveled and encountered all types of people and situations until finally they found the place. They made it to the point of destiny and the person they sought—but only to find that what they needed was already inside of them. No wizard could grant them what they were asking. No witch could block them from getting what they desired. And that, my friend, is the case of life.

Many times we search and hope to find what we desire, but we fail to stop and search within ourselves. We ask for courage without ever realizing that we have been handling challenges and performing courageous acts for years without ever giving ourselves credit. We ask for a brain (or better mindset), and all the time, we are the wisest component in the group. We are assets just waiting to be discovered, and there are directions to lead us to our destiny.

HE WILL GIVE YOU DEVINE DIRECTIONS

King David, the great psalmist penned the following excerpt as a portion of the longest chapter of the bible:

Teach me, O Lord, the way of Your statutes,
And I shall keep it to the end.
Give me understanding, and I shall keep Your law;
Indeed, I shall observe it with my whole heart.
Make me walk in the path of Your commandments,
For I delight in it.
Incline my heart to Your testimonies, And not to covetousness.
Turn away my eyes from looking at worthless things,
And revive me in Your way.

Establish Your word to Your servant,
Who is devoted to fearing You.
Turn away my reproach which I dread,
For Your judgments are good.

Psalm 119:33-39— New King James Version

Using this passage as a guiding text, David takes us on a tour and gives us an example on how we might seek and obtain directions for life's journey. I am convinced that we all start out on life's path with a clean slate and a will to do what is right and good. I do not believe that God who placed us here and orchestrated a plan for us to live prosperous and healthy lives, would wish that for us or design a destiny for us which we were not intended to attain. I am a firm believer, however that every step we take in life is critical to us achieving our ultimate destiny. Things don't just happen by chance while others things are deliberately done. I am also inclined to agree with those of the school of thought that the things which are manifested in our lives are the direct results of what we have created in our thoughts and desires. Each and every one of us, whether consciously or subconsciously have made plans for our lives; and we are taking small steps each day toward completing those plans.

Although life is a journey that every living creature must move through, no two people or beings have the same exact path. No matter how similar or close you are, no matter how connected you are to another, we all must take varying paths to get to our ultimate destiny. Even if some of us are on our way to the same point in our lives, some will arrive there quicker than others.

Those who are fortunate have already made it, but it's only because they thought about it more. They were clear in their minds that it was the only destination for them, so they've arrived.

But why is it taking you so long? Have you ever asked yourself that question? Why does it take some longer to get where we need to be? How is it that some people make it to their destiny seemingly with no struggle and in no time at all while others seem to be detoured? God knows we are trying to get to the place where He wants us, but how can we get there faster? Well, I think I may have the answer in response to what's taking you so long to arrive.

As I have shared earlier on, you've got to determine where you are as in your assessment. Oh come on, you've heard of the old adage, *"If you don't know where you are, then you can't know where you're going"*. Stop wondering aimlessly around, and make a vow to just get where you are going. Make a decision that you are going to get there. But you must also decide on where in the world is *there*, which is an additional point I want to make.

Before you can get *there*, you've got to decide where is *there.* Now I know it sounds confusing, but *there* may be a different place for all of us. *There* is determined by the one in pursuit, so you might see getting a college degree as success; and that is *there* for you. You must decide where you want to go, and only you can decide. Another passage of scripture cited in Proverbs 16:9, speaks to this case as well.

A man's heart plans his way: but the LORD directs his steps.

Proverbs 16:9

In other words, what it really teaches us is the following: You decide where you want to go. You decide what you really want out of life. You set your desires and destinations, but it is the LORD who directs your path. As I considered the implication of this reality, I began to ask the Lord a few questions. I asked Him questions like, "Why does it take some longer to get to their place of destiny? Why is it that you won't just take us to the place of promise in a shorter time?"

At this point, I also usually to remind the LORD of His power, and my conversations with Him usually form like this: "You are the Lord who keeps your promises. You are the Lord who teaches and causes us to prosper, and you are the giver of every good and perfect gift. I could be at point A today and point B by tomorrow, because I know that you have the power to do it.

So what's going on, God? What's *really* going on because inquiring minds want to know." And here is what He says to me: "Yes, I am all of those things that you said I am. I have kept every promise that I made to you, and I am the Lord thy God who teaches you to prosper. But have you been following my directions?"

Can you imagine how God is so awesome as to turn everything around and catch me with a question? So of course, I was immediately convicted. I tried not to answer the question. That didn't work because everything got real quiet as if God was waiting on my answer. And here's what I mustered up.

I started by confessing... "God I just messed up. I didn't do it because I didn't understand. I felt just like an ill-prepared pupil in a classroom confronted by my teacher. You know how the teacher starts asking questions, and you put your head down hoping not to be selected because you know that whatever answer you can offer will not be the right selection. Yes, the curriculum had been given, and the lessons had been taught, but I had not been paying attention.

Admittedly, God had given me directions time and time again, but I failed each time because I refused to listen. He was gracious enough to repeat Himself as He said to me, "Have you been following directions? You want to get *there*, and you want the good grade, but have you studied to show yourself approved?" He continued, "Do you know and keep my laws? Maybe, just maybe, it's taking you a little bit longer because you have not been disciplined enough to follow directions."

Often enough we have been shown the destination, but we won't get there because we don't know the way. Although He has revealed it, you can't just desire your way to it. You've got to be directed to it. Are you disciplined enough? Can you go through what you got to go through to get to *there*? Yes, *there* is a place of peace. *There* is the good life personified, but we keep asking ourselves...Are we there yet because we fail to get it. And here's where David helps us in Psalm 119.

Teach me, O LORD, the way of Your statutes;
and I shall keep it to the end.
Give me understanding, and I shall keep Your law;

Indeed, I shall observe it with my whole heart.
Make me walk in the path of Your commandments,
For I delight in it.

Psalm 119:33-35 — New King James Version

We all have desires, but we don't get to delight in our destiny until we do it His way. There is a righteous path, and if we follow it, He will make us rich and add no sorrow. If you would take your desire and couple it with the divine directions of the Lord, I am convinced He will direct your path. Choosing His straight and narrow path to your destiny, may take you a little longer to arrive, but it will be worth it when you get there. You should never compromise your morals, character, or integrity in efforts to speed up the process. I know so many people who do this, but I have always been able to witness their demise. Along their journey to succeed, they trample and step on others to get to the top (a place of *there*), and they soon lose everything. Relationships are broken and clients vanish as they learn of their unscrupulous acts. I have a word of advice for you...*DO IT RIGHT, AND YOU WILL BE ALRIGHT!* He will bring you quickly to your expected end just as He has for those who trust Him.

GET A PICTURE OF WHERE YOU'RE GOING

My husband and I once had the pleasure of vacationing in Hawaii to celebrate our 16th wedding anniversary. After contemplating for some time, we decided that this was the place we wanted to go. It was our desire to get there because we had heard so much about it. We had seen pictures of it, and several people who had gone before us, told us that we had to make it to this paradise. No pictures, no brochures, and no website would compare to what we would behold if we went there. Everybody was encouraging us as they told us of the endless shopping, great food, the calm, blue waters, and the plentiful palm trees. They were so happy for us to go to Hawaii because that was truly the place.

While they told us of all the wonderful aspects of the place, nobody mentioned the discomfort we would come to experience during the lengthy journey which was the airplane ride. Once we boarded the plane, we were able to view a digital map on the monitor which showed us where we were in relation to where we were going. The expected travel time was 9 hours, and we were shown pictures of this great paradise throughout the entire ride. The attendants gave us an abundance of instructions and directives throughout the flight, but nobody said how we could alleviate the jet lag we were going to feel later on. That's the part they omit.

Why am I making this point? Because they can show you a picture of where *there* is, but if they tell you everything about the trip, then you might change your mind about starting out. You might cause yourself to miss out on paradise if you knew what it took to get there. But if it's worth going to, you must go through what you got to go through to get to there.

So you have determined where you are. You have decided where you want to go, and you've been disciplined enough to start out with God's divine directions. When you follow that sequence, the only thing left to do is delight in your desire. Upon our arrival to Hawaii, we couldn't thank God enough for allowing our eyes to behold this beautiful land that so many call paradise. We were so glad that we had paid attention and learned from somebody who had gone before us. See that's vital to you getting to your destination faster too!

ASK SOMEBODY ELSE FOR DIRECTIONS

Learn from somebody else, and don't be afraid to ask them questions if you lose your way. I told you I like asking questions, but that is a quality others may lack. Be smart enough to pay attention and model after someone who has achieved some of the things you want to achieve. As an administrator, you might imagine how closely I work with my pastors. I am often in their presence to review vital information about ministry activities and the business of the church. I cannot afford to be afraid to ask questions. I also take this time to inquire about issues concerning my life or interests for which I desire further clarification. I want to know:

What does it mean when the bible says this?
Where can I get the information that I need?
What books are you reading now?
How many hours do you sleep at night?
How do you meet the demands of ministry?

I understand that they are spiritually mature, and they have been traveling a little longer on the same road I desire. I am always the student in their presence, and I want to learn the best way to achieve what I want to achieve. But I don't have to constantly call them or meet with them to learn these things. That is not what I am suggesting here. What I am suggesting is this. I learn from them by being at bible study and making the sacrifice to come to intercessory prayer which is where that information is being offered. It may take me longer to get it, but that's why I am there so often to hear what they have to say. I regard the Word of God from my pastors as if it's a spiritual navigation system. You have seen those speaking "Never Lost" devices contained within some vehicles. You program it by entering where you are and where you want to go, then miraculously the lady starts speaking..."Follow the highlighted route". She even tells you how long it should take, and she gives us the best way to go, but sometimes we still go against the directions.

In the event you make a wrong turn, she utters..."Re-calculating route". Which means— you messed up, but as soon and you can make a legal U-turn; get it right. It may take you longer, because you didn't follow the directions. But just keep driving, and you can figure this out. In the same way, God is saying, "Listen and follow the highlighted route and the vision that I've given to you. The voice is there to help you, and even though you got caught up— here's a detour. You may have been going left when I said right, but you can take another U-turn right here." Isn't it good to know you can get back on track again? If you just keep driving, eventually you will arrive, and it will all be worth it.

CHAPTER 12

NOW IS THE TIME

To be certain that you are in your *"Now"* season, you must experience overflow. Put away the notion of just enough. I believe there's somebody reading this, and you are like me. You may be saying…"I want everything God has for me." You believe that He wants to bless you BIG TIME. I also believe that He wants to bless us abundantly because He's a good God, and He wants to be good to us. If it is true that every good and perfect gift comes from Him, we have to remember that He wants us to win.

When we remember how good God has been, and the battles that He has caused us to win, it not only gives us reason to praise Him for what He's already done, but it gives us hope and compels us to believe Him for the next dimension. Just stop to think for a minute. If we could just remember the past victories and believe God to take us through the battle at hand, we can make it!

Now is the time to get your life in order so that the blessings and abundance of God can flow through to you. We cannot expect to be blessed beyond measure if our houses are not in order. If you are willing to take the time to assess, plan, intervene, and evaluate what is before you, riches and overflow will be the only result.

Just like the poor widow with the olive oil in the bible, we can get overflow during times of economic stress and uncertainty. When the prophet Elisha asked her the question, "What can I do to help you?" He was really setting her on a course to see how she could help herself. His next question was... "What do you have in the house?" And sadly enough, her answer was:

"Nothing at all, except a flask of olive oil." When you take the time to analyze her response, you see that she had disregarded something as priceless as olive oil, and you should realize the significance here. During that day, olive oil was worth a high price in her setting. And what she was inferring here is, "I have something of value, but it's not enough." She had only a flask (which is about a small glass full), but she regarded it as "nothing at all" as she did not see the true worth in it. Although it was just a little, nevertheless, she had "something" in her house.

Before we begin to judge this poor widow, I want to ask you the question:

What do you have in your house? I'm not referring to your physical house or residence this point, but I am talking about the house or the temple of the Holy Spirit. Your body is the temple, but what has He placed on the inside of you that you regard as "nothing at all". In this example, the oil represents the anointing, and no matter how much of it you have, you are still anointed. You possess something of value, and even though it's not as much as you may think, it's all in how you look at it. You can regard the glass as half full, or say the glass is half empty, but you've got a little "oil" or anointing in you.

Remember that little becomes much when you place it in the Master's hands. I may not have much, but what I do have...It's valuable, and I'm going to use it to bless the Lord. I'm going to live my life like it is golden and take what I have been given to create more. Now is the time for overflow!

WHAT DO YOU HAVE IN YOUR HOUSE?

What is your anointing? Do you know what you are anointed to do? Even as a child, I tried to find my true purpose, and it troubled me when I did not recognize what I was called to do. That was truly frustrating, but what is more frustrating is when you know what you are called to do, but you lock up your gift, and you think it isn't significant enough. Many have bottled their gifts and considered it to be "nothing at all". The widow felt as though she could not make a difference, so she resigned to being average failing to use her gift. People of today assume the same posture. Time and again, I have heard individuals say, "Nobody appreciates me", but I think to myself...YOU don't even appreciate you, so you go through life frustrated and always feeling like there must be something more. You're always searching for the more, but God says, "Until you realize what I've given you, and until you use what you have, you can't walk into abundance and financial freedom."

Naturally speaking, there is a treasure in your physical house as well. Those magazines may be a business in the making. The excess furniture or antique vase tucked in your attic may be converted into cash and used as capital or seed money for your business. Photograph it and place it online for sale. Ebay.com or Craigslist.com are well-known sites for achieving your re-sale objectives. If you are unsure of how to do it, get someone to help you with this endeavor and offer them a few bucks if it sells. The point to all of this is to encourage you to look for the treasure in your house. Maybe it's in the content of your closet or buried within your being. Nevertheless, there is something of value in your possession, and it is the abundance that awaits you.

So the widow tells Elisha that she has this oil in her house, and he then instructs her to go out and borrow as many empty jars as she can from her neighbors and friends. He challenges her to "do something". He tells her to go out and borrow as many empty jars as she can so that she can go into her house and pour out the olive oil she has in her flask into the many jars.

Now here's a point to get excited about. Do you know what the jars represent to me? The Lord showed me the jars she was instructed to borrow and revealed to me that the jars represent opportunity. She went out to do something as she acted in faith upon the word from the prophet. You may recognize that he was encouraging her to get outside of her box and venture out into other people's boxes. John C. Maxwell was accurate when he wrote, "Society wants to keep people in boxes. Most people are married to the status quo." So why not break out of your box and do something differently? Look for unique opportunities, and follow up on them.

Each jar that she collected was just another "opportunity" for her to pour out the oil. She filled jar after jar, and the oil continued to flow as long as she had empty jars. The oil continued to flow with each and every opportunity! He cautioned her to borrow jars, but to borrow not a few. I believe what he was trying to say here was this: "Think bigger!" Get rid of the notion of small-thinking because now is not the time to think small. John C. Maxwell also says in his *How Successful People Think*, "If you desire to seize new opportunities and open new horizons, then you need to add big-picture thinking to your abilities." Essential to your success, you must see pass where you are right now. See yourself driving what you want to drive and living where you want to live. Not just better...but bigger and better. If you are going to dream, you might as well dream bigger.

She was obedient to the word of the prophet, and her ***little*** became much as she poured. Firstly, she was blessed because she followed the directions. She did exactly as she was told, even though it seemed ridiculous. She filled one container after another, and here's the revelation. When you begin to value and pour out your anointing searching for opportunities to be a blessing, then and only then, will your life change. When you look for opportunities to pour out and give, then you can live in the overflow. She continued to pour as they kept the jars coming, and the oil kept flowing as long as there were containers. When you look for opportunities to pour out and give— even when you think that what you have isn't enough. God can't help but bless you.

As I focus on opportunities, I want to admonish you not to pass up your opportunity to give. Everything we have, and whatever we receive in money or material goods, or opportunities, or in the moments of each day— it is purely and simply a gift from God. It's an expression of His love, and evidence of His grace and favor. Every possession is entrusted to us to steward and enjoy and to use for His purposes. So don't miss your opportunity to sow into others. You may choose to give to your church, a charitable organization, or offer benevolence to someone in need. Even if you think that your gift is insignificant, you can still be a blessing through your obedience.

There was another widow who said to the prophet Elijah, "I only have a handful of flour, and a little cooking oil." She was gathering up a few sticks to cook her bread, eat it and die when the prophet approached her. He instructed her to go and prepare the little that she had, but to give it to him so that he might eat first. Afterward, there would be enough food for her and her son. He assured her that there would always be plenty of flour and oil left in her containers until the time when the LORD sends *rain* and the crops started to grow again!

So many times, we are challenged to give— even in the midst of our lack. Our pastors prompt us to sow into kingdom building by bringing the little that we have to them to let the LORD bless it. Instead of eating what little you have with a plan to later die, you might as well give it and be blessed. Instead of starving to death, allow God to use the seed that you have to bless you with an abundance of rain. I know it is easy and logical to hold onto it in your house, but why not bring it, and be blessed? Worth is gained in what we use, not in what we hold.

I am reminded of a story I once heard about an elderly woman who lived so poorly that everybody felt sorry for her. The house was a mess, and she dressed as though she was near homelessness. She often ate scraps and took every hand out that she could. As a matter of fact, she would stand at the door of the corner store and beg everyone who went in and out until finally one day, she died. Rumor has it, that when they searched her house, the family was startled to find the oddest "insulation" stuffed into the walls. There was money and all types of stocks and bonds tucked in every nook and crevice that she could find. There was also money behind pictures in the frames. If you didn't know, now you do...that's where your grandfather hides his money.

The story goes on to reveal... The old woman was rich in possessions, yet she lived so poorly because she did not use what was in her possession. She deliberately hoarded the things which could have made her life totally different. I imagine she had many opportunities to give, but she failed miserably, as she held on tightly to what she had failing to share or give anything. But as you read this passage, you should make up in your mind that you are going to

116

give because that's the only way you are going to get it. I am often challenged to give liberally, and many times, I don't have what I consider to be "enough". But I have purposed in my heart that I am going to give my way out of struggles. I currently search for opportunities to give because I know God is trying to get something to me. If my hand is closed when he passes, then I can't receive what he's giving.

Upon experiencing the greatest act of sale I could have as a realtor, I was greatly challenged to sow a huge seed. I was honored to find the land and property for my church's new site as we had outgrown our old church. After searching for the perfect location and deal, I was able to negotiate an awesome deal, and we secured the transaction. Shortly before the sale was finalized, my husband and I began to talk about giving the entire commission check back to the church. I was afraid to speak to him about what God was prompting me to do, but as it turns out... God was also speaking to him at the same time about the sacrifice to plant the largest seed we had ever planted. Did we need the money? You better believe we did, and it was a tremendous challenge of our faith. But I gave back the entire commission from the sale of our new building. Our pastors did not ask us to do it, and I think it would have been a little easier if they had because we would have obeyed their request had they just asked. Ultimately, I had to depend on the God in me. I had to listen to that inner voice speaking to me saying, "Give it, and give it all."

I had come to the conclusion that I was receiving a blessing, but it wasn't what I had asked for. I wanted so much more than I had in my hand, because it was a commission after a 4-way split. I had to be a good steward over what was in my hand. I could not complain about being challenged all the time to give over and beyond because I wanted a blessing that was "over and beyond". That's why I used the seed I had to get what I wanted. And no, I haven't gotten it yet, but I know that it's on the way. I've had some short days since I gave it, but I used it as my seed, and I know that the harvest has got to come. I sought out an *opportunity* to learn more about real estate, and now I am in a position to be knowledgeable enough to negotiate deals for His kingdom. Is that awesome, or what? I'm using the opportunity to pour out my gift, and when I'm done pouring out, there's going to be enough left over for me and my house. I'm giving away what I have in order to pay off my debts and have enough left over to live.

I want to live in the overflow like this widow with the flask of oil. If you are obedient enough to pour out, you can live in the overflow too. If you are obedient enough to give it away, you can reap abundance. Now is the time for reaping over and beyond what you may ask or think. Be obedient enough to go out searching for opportunities to pour out what you have been called to do. Then, and only then, will you live in the overflow.

IT'S ALWAYS A GOOD TIME TO INVEST

Now is the time to sow into what you want. No matter what you have to give or how little you think it may be... it is the time to invest something toward your goals. Maybe you have the dream of owning a home. Now is the time to start sowing a little each day toward that dream. Start by giving up your lunch, and put the $10 away in a safe place. Tell yourself that you have just started a savings for the new house you will soon purchase. Once you have done this only 3 times, you should go to the bank and open a checking or savings account with the $30. Tell them that you are planning to purchase a home, and you just need a place to save your money. I guarantee they will introduce you to a banking loan officer as a preliminary marketing measure. Be sure to take their card and ensure them that you will be back to discuss home loan options with them once you have enough in your account. Who knows where this one encounter will take you. You may learn of some special program they are offering for first time home buyers. The bank might even have a special savings interest rate for those who are saving in preparation for home ownership. They might also give you a list of bank foreclosures, and advise you on purchasing a home with little or no down payment if you are interested in purchasing a pre-foreclosed home. All of this can happen just as a result of opening an account with the bank. You are now in a relationship with someone greater and more knowledgeable about what you want. What's more, when you opened the account, you just created an opportunity. You just obtained a vessel through which God can pour wealth. You want abundance, but there must be a place to store it once it starts to flow into your hands.

Maybe times are tough now, but when you are willing to search for opportunities, you will find them. When you are prepared to receive opportunities, they will come to you. That is exactly how I did it while going after my goals. I decided to take one step at a time, and sow a little of what I had in order to take advantage of every opportunity. Some goals seem as though they are too difficult to attain, but you should take one small step at a time so you can achieve great goals. Let's say you want to start a property management business. Taking small, focused steps will start you on your path to success.

Here are 12 small steps to help you get started:

Step #1: Go online: search for keyword *"property management"* in your state and review other property management businesses to determine what they currently offer

Step #2: Locate courses/online products related to property management

Step #3: Determine if there are any certification requirements or real estate courses necessary to open a property management company

Step #4: Draft a simple business plan incorporating your goals for the business

Step #5: Contact/Visit a business attorney to legally incorporate your business

Step #6: Once you have your business articles and tax identification number, open a bank account for your business

Step #7: Visit the small business administration office to apply for a small business loan

Step #8: Go online to locate/purchase property management software

Step #9: Purchase office supplies/equipment to organize files in your office

Step #10: Visit a print shop to order business cards and flyers to promote your business

Step #11: Create a website advertising your business content

Step #12: Tell everyone you know about your new business venture

These small steps will work for most any business idea you may have, and they will lead to a successful start. Now is the time to make it happen. Whatever your dream, whatever your desire—taking small steps toward the goals will bring you to your expected end. Realize your personal potential, and make the commitment to get through whatever you need to go through in order to win. Tap into whatever you have left, and do the things that will make it work.

One of the best quotes I have ever read states: "The best way to get it done is to get started." Now is the time to stop procrastinating, as there is no logical reason to wait for anything further. Start with what you have and what you know. Now is the time to act upon what we have given you within the pages of this book to move forward without delay. NOW is the time to achieve whatever you desire!

NOTES

Franklin, Jentezen. *Believe That You Can*. Florida: Charisma House, 2008.

Gardner, Chris. *Start Where You Are: Life Lessons in Getting From Where You Are to Where You Want to Be*. New York: Harper Collins Publishers, 2009.

Maxwell, John. *How Successful People Think: Change Your Thinking, Change Your Life*. New York: Center Street, 2009.

Orman, Suze. *The 9 Steps to Financial Freedom: Practical & Spiritual Steps So You Can Stop Worrying*. New York: Crown Publishers, 1997.

Ramsey, Dave. *The Total Money Makeover: A Proven Plan for Financial Fitness*. Tennessee: Thomas Nelson, 2003, 2007.

Sutton, Garrett. *The ABC's of Getting Out of Debt: Turn Bad Debt Into Good Debt and Bad Credit Into Good Credit*. New York: Time Warner Book Group, 2004.

Vaynerchuk, Gary. *Crush It!* New York: Harper Collins Publishers, 2009.

Vitale, Joe. *The Attractor Factor*. 2nd Ed. New Jersey: John Wiley & Sons, Inc., 2008.

The Economist, The chaos after Greece's rescue: Coming to a City Near You? May 8-10th, 2010.

Success. How Positive Attitude Boosts Physical Health. May 2010.